BADGES OF BONDAGE

The Conquest of the Sikh Mind (1847-1947)

Singh Sahib Guru Fatha
Singh Khalsa

CONTENTS

Title Page	
Preface (1996)	6
Preface (2021)	8
Illustrations	10
Introduction	16
I – The Sikhism of Subservience	21
II – The Face of the Guru	31
III – Dressing for Imperialism	41
IV – Her Majesty's Purveyors of Narcotics	47
V – The Jobs of the English	54
VI – Colonial Justice	62
VII – A British Education	67
VIII – Conclusion: "Angrezeemat"	75
Epilogue	83
Notes	86
Glossary	100
Bibliography	104

About the Author:

Singh Sahib Guru Fatha Singh Khalsa is a teacher, writer, social activist and agent of change. He embarked on the path of Gursikh Yoga in Canada at the age of 18. In the late 1970s, he launched two important human rights case. One allowed turbaned and bearded Sikhs to serve in the Canadian Armed Forces. The other permitted bearded Sikhs, Muslims and Jews to serve in the transportation industry in Ontario.

Guru Fatha Singh has taught Kundalini Yoga as taught by Yogi Bhajan for most of his life. Guru Fatha Singh's articles have been published by *The Globe and Mail, The Sikh Review, Vitality Magazine* and *Sikhnet.com*. His serious writing began in 1996 with the self-publication of *Badges of Bondage*.

More books are in the works for publication with Kindle/Amazon Books. These include: *The Essential Gursikh Yogi: The Yoga and Yogis in the Past, Present and Future of Sikh Dharma; Five Paragons of Peace: Magic and Magnificence in the Guru's Way;* and *Messenger from the Guru's House: The Life and Legacy of Siri Singh Sahib Harbhajan Singh Khalsa Yogiji "Yogi Bhajan."*

With Farah Jindani, PhD, Guru Fatha Singh is the co-author of two published academic papers: "A Journey to Embodied Healing: Yoga as a Treatment for Post-Traumatic Stress Disorder" (2015) and "A Yoga Intervention Program for Patients Suffering from Symptoms of Posttraumatic Stress Disorder: A Qualitative Descriptive Study" (2015). To keep up with Guru Fatha Singh's current essays, videos, projects, or to connect, visit: gurufathasingh.com

Praise for Badges of Bondage

"Thoughtful people everywhere will be touched by Guru Fatha Singh's concern, as also benefit from a reading of his first book. His first set of documented writing, succinct and neatly produced, explore the Sikh faith through history. His loyalty to the Guru's purpose is firm as a rock. His understanding of Gurbani is extraordinarily perceptive, and their rendering into English sensitively poetic. His objective in compiling the historic panorama is to re-awaken the true spirit of the Khalsa."
Sardar Saran Singh, editor, *The Sikh Review,* Kolkata

"Your essay makes very cogent reading and I enjoyed going through it. Your narration is powerful and effective." *Professor* Harbans Singh, *The Encyclopedia of Sikhism,* Punjabi University, Patiala

"The author rightly laments the surrender of the rich spiritual heritage of Sikhism to the so-called secular, materialistic and dehumanizing values of the West planted during British rule." *Sardar* Gurcharan Singh, *Abstracts of Sikhism,* Chandigarh

"I am writing on behalf of the Siri Singh Sahib. The Siri Singh Sahib really enjoyed reading your book and was appreciative of the work that you have put in. You seem to have done considerable research which is well-documented. I also found your writing style comfortable to read, and it held my interest throughout. I felt your approach is sound, for while it does not actually point fingers and place blame, it makes clear that Sikhs themselves are accountable and responsible for their circumstances." *Singh Sahib* Gurutej Singh Khalsa, Founder, *Akal Security*

All rights reserved. No part of this work covered by the copyrights hereon may be reproduced or used in any form or by any means —graphic, electronic or mechanical, including photocopying, recording, taping or information and retrieval systems—without the prior written permission of the author.

Khalsa, Guru Fatha Singh, 1954-

Badges of Bondage: The Conquest of the Sikh Mind 1847-1947 C.E.

Published 1996, 1998, 2021

ISBN 978-0-9682658-0-2

Acknowledgements

Thanks overall is due to Waheguru – without Whom, what is possible? My gratitude also for Siri Singh Sahib Harbhajan Singh Khalsa Yogiji, who set me on this path, and to Sant Baba Darshan Singh Ji, who allowed me the time and facilities to concentrate fully on the work at hand.

Thanks also to Sardar Harinder Singh Chopra, Assistant Librarian. Bhai Gurdas Library, Guru Nanak Dev University, for his overview and assistance in locating resource materials for this subject, Doctor Baldev Singh of Ludhiana for his helpful recollections on the early merchandising of tea in Punjab, and Professor Sukhdev Singh Sol, Guru Nanak Dev University for his insights on some economic aspects of imperialism in Punjab.

"Who wins the mind, wins all!"
Guru Nanak Dev Ji (from Japji Sahib)

"The most powerful weapon in the
hands of the oppressor
is the mind of the oppressed."

Steve Biko – martyr for the cause of freedom
(South Africa 1946-1977 C.E.)

PREFACE (1996)

For those who love the Khalsa of Guru Gobind Singh and the pure, unfettered vision of Guru Nanak, the study of the colonial subjugation of the Sikh nation is not a pretty read. It is the thesis of this essay that colonization was a fundamental spiritual defeat for the Sikh nation, and that Sikhs everywhere still labour under the trauma of it, though independence from India was achieved fifty years ago.

There are those who would see in Hindus a ready-made scapegoat for the weaknesses and deficiencies among Sikhs today. However, considering the generous spirit of Guru Nanak Dev, this author has concluded that a more fruitful course can be found in a thorough self-examination, a look within to see where the vestiges of one hundred years of imperial domination still hurt, still hamper outward expression and internal sovereignty.

To whine and complain about the afflictions suffered during the colonial era would be very unSikhlike. The Sikh nation has borne the inevitable with a spirit of stoic resignation. However, the dysfunctionality observable today in the conduct of the Panth's affairs – visible in some of its significant details and in its impact (or lack thereof) on the world at large – betrays the crippling effects of a festering wound deep within. The promise of Khalsa is splendid beyond comparison, yet so long as this condition is not treated, it poisons our present and future prospects. In the interest of removing this long-festering malignancy, the present work has commenced.

If the procedure releases a geyser of puss and fetid aroma, or reveals some aspect had hoped rather not to see, this humble and inexperienced surgeon apologizes for the discomfort.

Unfortunately, considering the infection's advanced stage of development, hardly any more experienced doctor was willing to undertake such an intrusive exercise. Most were content to accept the unacceptable, designating the excruciating agony a "routine discomfort," while they anticipated declaring the inevitable outcome of their inaction "death by natural causes." This humble surgeon hopes the necessary faults and inadequacies of such a work as this might be forgiven, and that others, more worthy than himself, might be moved to carry this critical, self-healing work to its necessary conclusion.

PREFACE (2021)

With the passage of time, a student of the history becomes a player in the unfolding course of their own history. This has been my privilege, living in two centuries. Really, it has been a life of privilege for unlike so many whose names have filled the books of our history, my sacrifices have been minor. I have shed no blood and spent not a night in prison.

When this book first was published, it was not quite fifty years after the end of the British Raj. Since that publication, nearly a quarter century has passed. Much has changed and much has remained the same. Some excellent books on Sikh studies, even a couple of encyclopedias, have been published.

While this is not the occasion for a detailed study, it is remarkable and inspiring to see how the turban has made its mark in East and West. In both hemispheres, young Sikh women are coming up with the habit of crowning themselves with graceful turbans. It is a good thing for it would appear there is a race on now with many Muslim women visibly and openly crowning themselves as well. This is a time when a woman can be proud of her religious heritage and the world generally is increasingly accepting of that fact.

Where once Prime Minister Manmohan Singh was an outlier, a lonely figure on the global stage, turbaned men today are cropping up positions of public office in the West as never before. In the USA, once described by poet Leonard Cohen as "the cradle of the best and the worst," a Sikh sardar served as mayor of Charlottesville, Virginia from 2012-15. In France, polarized between its native Gauls and its visible immigrant communities, Ranjit Singh Goraya has improbably been elected deputy mayor of Bobibny, population 53,000, a suburb in the outskirts of Paris. In Canada, since 2017, Jagmeet Singh has served as the leader of Canada's fourth-ranking national party. The country's minister of defence, Harjit Sajjan, has served with the ruling Liberal Party since 2015.

In Great Britain, once a haven of cultural assimilation, visible Sikhs are increasingly taking up public roles in academia, business, entertainment, sports, and philanthropy. Perhaps none is as loved and admired as Ravi Singh, founder and CEO of Khalsa Aid International, which has rescued Englanders from floods, and offered assistance also in Iraq, Lebanon, Indonesia, India, Kenya, and elsewhere.

In the realm of spiritual outreach, Siri Singh Sahib Harbhajan Singh Khalsa Yogiji passed in 2004, but not before establishing his life's dream, Miri Piri Academy just outside Amritsar. Students from six continents come to MPA inspired by its seva programs at Harimandir Sahib, its robust discipline and comradery, and its Sikh ambience. Meanwhile, the seeds of Sikh dharma have sprouted now in China, Russia, Europe, Africa, Australia, North and South America. Hardly a country has not been touched.

There is work to do, of course. It is one thing for singular individuals to hold political office, to provide humanitarian aid, or offer classes in a holistic and empowering lifestyle. It is quite another to strive and collaborate as a global community united and dedicated to the good of all. May Waheguru guide and bless us in service and unity!

ILLUSTRATIONS

Plate 1: Painting of the Battle of Ferozeshah by Charles Stewart Hardinge, 1845

Plate 2: "Palace at Lahore" (actually Ranjit Singh's tomb), a wood engraving by E. Therond, published in 'Le Tour du Monde', 1888

Plate 3: Photograph of the Gothic Cathedral-style clock tower in Amritsar by unknown artist, 1860's

Plate 4: Painting of an investiture ceremony by King George V of a raja during the 1911 Delhi Durbar by George Percy Jacomb-Hood, circa 1913

Plate 5: *Gutka,* or meditation book, of Maharani Jindan Kaur by unknown artist, 1828-1830

Plate 6: Photograph of Maharaja Duleep Singh by Dr. Ernst Becker, 1854

Plate 7: Late 19th century representation of Guru Nanak, his holy successors and his disciples,

Bhai Bala and Bhai Mardana by unknown artist, no date

Plate 8: "The Creation of Adam" by Michelangelo, 1508-1512

Plate 9: "God Judging Adam" by William Blake, 1795

Plate 10: Photograph of Khalsa Sikh couple wearing Guru's Bana by Gurvindergpk, 2019, Creative Commons Licence 4.0

Plate 11: Photograph of Bhangra dancing in festive Punjabi attire by Supreet Malhi, 2017, Creative Commons Licence 4.0

Plate 12: Etching of English couple wearing fashionable Victorian attire by unknown artist, 1859

Plate 13: Photograph of Edwin Samuel Montagu and an associate in top hats and tail coat by unknown artist, 1910's

Plate 14: Photograph of Assamese tea plantation workers being paid by European by Bourne & Shephard, 1903 or earlier

Plate 15: Lithograph of a drawing by W. S. Shergill of a drying room in an opium factory in Bihar, circa 1850

Plate 16: Photograph of a late 19th century train from Sialkot, Punjab to Jammu by unknown artist, no date

Plate 17: Photograph of the opening of the Rupar canal in 1882 by unknown artist, 1882

Plate 18: Photograph of men of the Regiment of Ludhiana by unknown artist, circa 1860

Plate 19: Postcard showing Sikh soldiers marching on their arrival in Marseilles by unknown artist, circa 1914

Plate 20: Photograph of courthouse in Gujranwala by unknown artist, 1865

Plate 21: Photograph of Amritsar Town Hall by Shankar S., Imposing entrance arch to the Town Hall- Partition Museum in Amritsar (24074291387).jpg, 2017, Creative Commons Licence 2.0

Plate 22: Painting of the execution of 65 Namdhari Sikhs in Malerkotla, Punjab by Vasily Vereshchagin, circa 1884

Plate 23: Photograph of Lahore High Court in the 1880's by unknown artist, no date

Plate 24: Photograph of church in Murree by Samuel Bourne, 1860

Plate 25: Photograph of government school in Amritsar by unknown artist, 1870

Plate 26: Photograph of Khalsa College by Joe mon bkk, 2019, Creative Commons Licence 4.0

Plate 27: Photograph of festive Punjabi food by Sunil Kumar Balu, 2015, Creative Commons Licence 4.0

Plate 28: Photograph of traditional English Sunday lunch by adactio, 2005, www.adactio.com.

Plate 29: Photograph of Jallianwala Bagh memorial, Amritsar by Bijay Chaurasia, 2016, Creative Commons Licence 4.0

Plate 30: Photograph of boy and dog in the Bengal famine of 1943 by unknown artist, 1943

Plate 31: Photograph of emergency trains crowded with desperate refugees by unknown artist, 1947

Plate 32: Government map of Punjab from *Imperial Gazetteer of India, Volume I* (1909)

1739 C.E.

"Who are these barbarians who challenge us with such impunity?"

"They are a group of holy men who come to visit the sacred waters of Amritsar twice a year, then disappear into nowhere."

"Where do they live?"

"They live on the saddles and eat as they run. They sleep on the backs of their galloping horses. We tyrannize over them and they find peace in it. One man fights like a hundred, and they are not afraid to die."

"Be forewarned! These rebels are destined to rule."[1]

> The above conversation is traditionally believed to have taken place between Nadir Shah of Persia, who several times led armies across Punjab on the way to plunder Delhi, and Zakriya Khan, the governor of Lahore.

1845 C.E.

In the battle of Pherooshahar (Ferozeshah), on 21st December… the Sikh soldiers, who had gone without food rations and who had been deprived of their reserve munitions through treachery, inflicted such heavy and crushing losses on the enemy that… the British high command had formally decided to "surrender unconditionally before the Sikh army."[2]

> From an account of the battle in which, according to the British governor-general, a man of much military experience, "the fate of India shook in the balance".(i)

1988 C.E.

The Sikhs' self-image bears little resemblance to reality... At times it appears that perhaps the Khalsa have run the course of history prescribed for them and that their Gurus in their inscrutable wisdom have given them leaders who will fulfill their death wish.[3]

> Taken from a synopsis of the situation facing Sikhs today, by historian and social commentator, Khushwant Singh.

INTRODUCTION

No nation gladly gives up its sovereignty, and none happily suffers subjugation. In order to achieve and maintain its dominance, the conquering power resorts to a number of stratagems to weaken the population it aims to govern. Some are subtle and long-term in their effect. Others are brutal and their results more immediate. Some stratagems are economic. Some are political. Some are military. All of them are psychological, for their intent is to intimidate and mold the consciousness of their victims in such a way as to make them governable and useful to the new regime.

Among people whose sovereignty has been taken from them, three psychological strategies for adjusting to the new reality are to be found. The first is to "knuckle under", disowning one's traditional values and aspirations in favour of those of the newly dominant culture. The second strategy is to avoid the painful humiliation of the present by focusing elsewhere, by dreaming instead of some idealized past or future when things were, or will be, as one thinks they "ought to be". The third approach is to "lick one's wounds" and come to grips with the current reality using, whenever possible, the strengths of the oppressor to empower the oppressed. When this strategy takes root among a significant portion of the people, that people ceases being "conquered", and becomes capable, once more, of determining its own destiny. Among Sikhs, even today, there are examples of each of these strategies to observe. The third option has yet to come into its own.

To fully appreciate the impact of the era of British rule in

Punjab, it is useful to have some perspective. Well before the arrival of the "angrezees", the Sikhs of Punjab had governed themselves according to the principles of "panchayat" and "Gurmatta" laid down for them by Guru Gobind Singh. To decide on matters of local concern, five respected Khalsa would meet to arrive at a consensus. The Khalsa, in its early years, also acknowledged the edicts issued by Banda Singh Bahadur, appointed by the Tenth Master as the military commander of the Khalsa, (1708-1716 C.E.), and Guru Gobind Singh's two surviving wives, Mata Sahib Dewan and Mata Sundri.

In the 1748 C.E., the Sikhs formed themselves into a confederacy of local groupings called "missals". All the missals, collectively known as "Sarbat Khalsa", met twice a year before the Akal Takhat to decide issues of general interest. Important matters were always resolved, there and elsewhere, in the presence of Siri Guru Granth Sahib. The decisions of these councils were known as "Gurmattas". This is how the Khalsa governed itself to the start of Maharaja Ranjit Singh's reign in 1801 C.E.

Through the force of arms and skillful diplomacy, the political realm of the Khalsa expanded considerably during the days of the great Sikh maharaja. As a result, the raj came to include large numbers of Moslems and Hindus. Maharaja Ranjit Singh worked to ensure fairness and reasonable representation for the interests of each community. In order to reflect the newly diversified culture of the Sikh state, the political aspect of these gatherings of the Khalsa in Amritsar at Baisakhi and Diwali was suspected from 1805 C.E.

With the demise of Ranjit Singh in 1839 C.E., the Sikh nation entered a period of palace intrigue, assassination, and political instability. Princes Kharak Singh, Naonihal Singh and Sher Singh, in quick succession, tried to manage an increasingly unmanageable situation.

While the Sikh royal house crumbled, the army gained in influence and authority. In effect, no one could rule without the army's support. The soldiers, for their part, were tired of being used in the course of seemingly endless aristocratic bloodletting and political maneuvering. They instituted panchayat councils as a means of functioning, independent of the palace coteries, in the name of Khalsa. From September 1843 C.E., with ascension of the seven-year-old maharaja, Dalip Singh, the term "Sarbat Khalsa" came to be used in the official correspondence of the Darbar. The terms "Sarkar Khalsa Ji" and "Khalsa Panth" also came to be used.(ii)

By the 21st of September, 1845 C.E., the Khalsa army had assumed full control of the government. Unfortunately, by then, anarchy, factionalism and treason had taken a heavy toll on the goodwill and resources accorded to the state. In November of that year, the Sarbat Khalsa gathered once more before the Akal Takhat, this time to make the fateful decision to militarily oppose the incursions of the British along the Sutlej River. The army offered up a stiff resistance to the "ferengees", costing the British a greater effort and heavier casualties than they had suffered in their conquest of the whole of India outside Punjab, but by February it was all over.

The angrezees exacted a punishing peace from the Punjab. The Darbar was forced to give up its claim to Kashmir, and to cede the Jullundar Doab and both sides of the Sutlej to the British. It was also forced to reduce the size of its army and hand over all guns that had been used in the war. Moreover, a large war indemnity was expected, to pay for the expense of waging war on the Sikh kingdom. British agents were stationed in Lahore, Jullundur, and Hazar/Deerajat to oversee the interests of the foreigners. Adding insult to injury, the erstwhile kingdom was sectioned into four judicial districts, each with a British judge and troops on hand to enforce his orders.

In November of 1848 C.E., many sections of the former Khalsa nation rose up against the ferengees in a desperate bid for a return to independence. The common soldiery put up a gallant fight, but their leaders, Tej Singh and Lal Singh, had long since made peace with the British, so the army hardly stood a chance. By March 14, they had surrendered their swords, and the British colonials set out to do what many of its officers had originally intended: annex the Punjab.

Plate 1   The British camp in the Battle of Ferozeshah

(Wikipedia: Battle of Ferozeshah [accessed 06/01/21])

I – THE SIKHISM OF SUBSERVIENCE

Guru Nanak Dev Ji -

In this Dark Age, there is no experience of God.
The way of sacredness is not known.
Holy places are desecrated and the world goes to ruin.
In this age, the Name of God is the Remedy.
The mean-spirited just close their eyes, plug their
noses, and pretend to be lost in meditation.

• • • • • • •

Once they had taken possession of Punjab, the angrezees set about reorienting their final Indian conquest, so that the interests it served were their own. Through the political genius of the British governor-general, Lord Dalhousie, the formerly independent Sikh nation was transformed into a hybrid colonial entity with its loyalties divided between its glorious past and the present interests of the imperial authority vested in Great Britain.

Dalhousie was a master of symbolic gestures. His government had the mausoleum of Punjab's one great maharaja embellished as a memorial to its bygone royal heritage. At the same time, the governor-general replaced the popular Nanakshahi coinage which had originated in the revolutionary days of Banda Singh Bahadur. In its place, the government provided the people with a colonial currency, made of cheaper metal. On it, was the image of the angrezee queen.[4]

One of the most remarkable examples of how the proud and independent Sikh spirit was remolded to serve the imperial interest could be seen in the Khalsa Army. From 1847 to 1857 C.E., Tej Singh, who had so ignobly betrayed his countrymen in time of war, set about reorganizing this once formidable foe of angrezee raj. Through his efforts, this fighting force was transformed into a willing instrument of the colonial power, to be used whenever and wherever it should see fit.[5]

By the time they arrived in Punjab, the British were well-practised in the art of rewarding their friends and providing formidable disincentives for those whose interests they found inimical with their own. The government gave land and official appointments to its supporters. Those the government wanted to discourage, faced the prospect of being deprived of their land holdings and being left with only a British government pension to live on. Hundreds of the angrezee raj's newest subjects were in this way directly shown the favour or disfavour of the new masters of the land.

One example stands out for special notice. Bhai Jawahar Singh was the son of the legendary general of the Sikh raj, Hari Singh Nalwa. During the wars with the British, Jawahar Singh had fought with distinction and exceptional determination. The government was so incensed that it took away his lands and refused him even a pension to live on. In contrast, Tej Singh the traitor was given a landed estate with an income of 90,000 rupees for the rest of his life.[6]

In one way or another, more than half the former Sikh ruling class had been dispossessed by the turn of the century. The government kept informed of the fortunes of the aristocracy, and showed itself more than willing to prop up those who supported it. There was no shortage of land to reward spies, agents, and the so-called "moderate Sikhs" who cooperated with the regime. Along with the former estates of those who had been dispossessed by the British, about ten million acres of formerly arid land had been brought under cultivation through canalization. These were all distributed among friends of the colonial government.

The holy Gurudwaras of the Sikhs were not exempt from the political meddling of the British. The angrezee legal system made the traditional custodians of the temples the owners of the Gurudwara buildings and the revenue-yielding lands associated with them. Many of these custodians, or "mahants", soon became out of control. In effect, they were no longer accountable to anyone. Some mahants began to discourage the congregations' participation in any aspect of Gurudwara management. They encouraged "moortee poojaa" in the temples, which were profitable but non-Sikh, and acquired personal habits, such as sexual licentiousness, which were objectionable to the Sikh congregations. Some enterprising custodians began to sell off Gurudwara lands for their own personal gain. Despite complaints from the Sikh communities, the British consistently sided with the mahants. The Government attitude toward the prospect of responsible management of the Sikh Gurudwaras is reflected in the following official communique.

My dear Lord Rippon,
It would be politically dangerous to allow the arrangement of Sikh temples to fall into the hands of a committee emancipated from Government control, and I trust Your Excellency will assist to pass such Orders in the case as will enable to continue the system which has worked out successfully for more than thirty years. Believe me.
        Sincerely yours,
        R.E. Egerton
        Lieutenant-Governor, Punjab
        Simla, 8th August, 1881[7]

By 1919 C.E., the extent to which Gurudwaras had come to serve the interests of the ferengees was revealed in a shocking and macabre light. Shortly after General Dyer had committed the widely condemned massacre of hundreds of unarmed men, women and children at Jallianwala Bagh in Amritsar, Arur Singh, the man appointed by the British to look after the affairs of the Golden Temple, invited the general and his assistant, Captain Briggs, to come to the holiest shrine of the Sikh Dharma to be honoured and initiated into the Order of Khalsa! On April 21 of that year, the following dialogue was recorded between Arur Singh, along with the priests of Harimandir and Akal Takhat, and the infamous general.

> "Sahib," they said, "you must become a Sikh even as Nikalseyan became a Sikh."
> The general thanked them for the honour, but objected that he could not, as a British officer, let his hair grow long.
> Arur Singh laughed. "We will let you off the long hair," he said.
> General Dyer offered another objection. "But I cannot give up smoking."
> "That you must do!" said Arur Singh.
> "No," said the general, "I am very sorry, but I cannot give up smoking."
> The priests conceded, "We will let you give it up gradually."
> "That I promise you," said the general, "at the rate of one cigarette a year."[8]

The shameless conduct of the temple management in the Dyer affair illustrated for everyone just how low these government agents would stoop to preserve their relationship with their foreign masters. Even the British later reprimanded Dyer and transferred him out of Punjab for ordering the mass murder in the holy city.(i) Within a short time, Sikhs everywhere rose up in revulsion. By 1925, through a determined campaign of non-violent demonstrations, which claimed the lives of some 400 martyrs, the Sikh nation had forced the colonial regime to give up its control of the major Gurudwaras.

Significantly, however, those Sikh leaders who took charge

of the Gurudwaras in the 1920's had become so Westernized overtime that they rejected the Sikh traditions of self-government, and adopted the British model instead. As a result, rather than being reverentially managed on the basis of consensus, panchayat and Gurmatta, the temples soon became staging grounds for Western-style democracy with all its inherently alienating customs of grand-standing, personal idolatry, and jostling for power.(ii)

The Harimandir has always been a powerful symbol of Sikh aspirations. By the time the Shiromani Gurdwara Parbandhak Committee began to manage it on behalf of all Sikhs, the Golden Temple had long since been fitted with electrical fixtures according to the modern Western custom. All day, kirtan was broadcast over loudspeakers, and at night the Harimandir assumed an electrical incandescence.

Two hundred thousand people had witnessed the occasion when the key and accounts of Harimandir Sahib were handed over to Sikh representatives by the colonial commissioner of Amritsar. The following summer, tens of thousands of Sikhs, Hindus and Moslems had removed the silt that had accumulated in the sarovar since the time of the great Sikh maharaja. Still the dark psychic sludge of more than seventy years of spiritual and political disempowerment remained largely undisturbed.

Plate 2   The tomb of Maharaja Ranjit Singh

Plate 3 Construction of the Gothic Cathedral-style clock tower seen behind Harimandir Sahib was completed in 1874. Built on the grounds of the maharaja's palace which the British had briefly repurposed as a missionary school, then a police station, jail and court house, and then demolished, it was a deliberate afront to local sensibilities. Rising above every other landmark, it brandished that quintessential Western invention, a clock with an illuminated dial to inspire a mechanized sense of timeliness and order across its domain. The tower was demolished in 1945 to allow for expansion of the marble walkway around Harimandir Sahib. In 1947, the SGPC management saw fit to build its own clock house at an entrance to the Golden Temple complex. (sikhmuseum.com, livehistoryindia.com [accessed 30/12/20])

Plate 4   An investiture ceremony by King George V of a raja during the Delhi Durbar, held December 7-16, 1911. This event showcased an intricate system of hierarchy and symbolism for the hundreds of royal states that existed precariously under the British Raj. According to the status they were given by the Raj, the semi-autonomous kingdoms were each permitted a symbolic gun salute. By this system, Patiala and Bahawalpur were granted 17-gun salutes, while Jind, Kapurthala and Nabha were given 13-gun salutes, and Malerkotla an 11-gun salute. By comparison, the King-Emperor of India, George V, was accorded a 101-gun salute at the Delhi Durbar of 1911. (Grewal & Banga [2018]; Wikipedia: Delhi Durbar, Salute state [accessed 30/12/20])

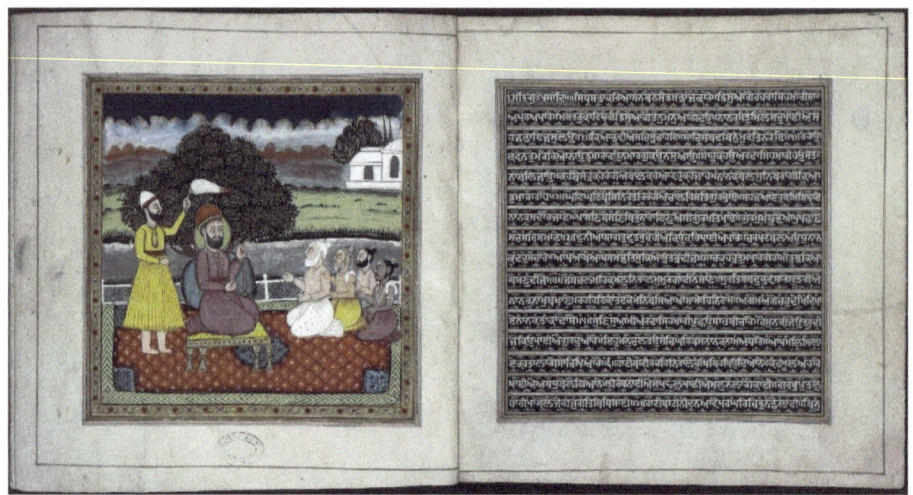

Plate 5 This Gutka, or meditation book, of Maharani Jindan Kaur (1817-1863), mother of Maharaja Daleep Singh, the last monarch of the Kingdom of Punjab remained with her from 1830. The Gutka contains Guru Nanak's Sidh Gosht, his dialogue with Sidh Yogis, and Guru Arjan's Bavan Akhari and Sukhmani. This is an example of the looting of priceless treasures of Punjab by the British. (Wikipedia: Maharani Jind Kaur [accessed 16/01/21]; British Library: Rani Jindan Prayer Book [accessed 31/12/20]) 31/12/20])

Plate 6   A photograph of Maharaja Duleep Singh (1838-1893) in England in 1854. He reigned, with his mother Maharani Jind Kaur as Regent, from 1843-1849. The colonial rulers imprisoned his mother in 1848, then deposed and kept the maharaja confined at Fatehpur, Uttar Pradesh, where he was to have no Indian visitors other than trusted servants and to be anglicized in every possible way. Under the influence of his long time Christian servant, Duleep Singh converted to Christianity in 1853 and left India to live in England in 1854. The maharaja arranged to rejoin his mother and bring her to England in 1861. He rejected Christianity and reverted to his Sikh family heritage in 1886. (Wikipedia: Maharaja Duleep Singh [accessed 03/01/21])

II – THE FACE OF THE GURU

Guru Arjun Dev Ji -

Your face is so beautiful, and the Sound of Your Words brings comfort and peace.

Guru Gobind Singh Ji -

Khalsa is my Special Form. I live in the Khalsa.

• • • • • • • •

Just as Guru Nanak's inspired genius coined a dharma, or way of life, for humanity, so Guru Gobind Singh gave that living dharma a unique and timeless human expression in terms of "five K's", the most visible and instantly recognizable of which is the "kes", or hair. Today, the unshorn, graceful tresses of Sikh women, and the natural long hair and beards of Sikh men frame a living belief in the divine possibility that breathes in everyone.

In this instance, the turban is not a cultural emblem. It can be wrapped and worn in any of a number of ways, according to the personality of the wearer. The turban can also be formed of any natural fabric of any national origin, and dyed or patterned in any of an infinite variety of styles and colours. It is simply a dignified and most practical accessory to the uncut hair on the head of the practising Sikh. Similarly, the shining face of a Khalsa(i) framed within the timeless context of their God-given crown of hair – and in the case of a man, his beard – may be of any age and race, ethnic and geographic origin.

About the evocative spiritual symbolism of the beard, the Encyclopaedia Britannica states:

The bearded races of mankind have commonly held the beard in high honour. It is the sign of full manhood... Adam, the primal man, and the deity and prophets of many faiths have been traditionally pictured with beards, as we were kings and nobles and dignitaries... In India and Turkey, the beard was allowed to grow as a symbol of dignity and wisdom... among Turks, slaves were shaved as a mark of servility.[9]

The full-bearded heritage of Christianity is vividly represented in Michelangelo's renowned fresco on the ceiling of the Sistine Chapel, where God and man are equally represented with white, flowing locks tumbling from their dignified faces.(ii) Man and God are similarly depicted in the visionary art of William Blake. The traditional encompasses Abraham and Moses and Jesus Christ himself. In modern times, it is continued by the widely popular "Santa Claus", an updated and largely fantasized version of Saint Nicholas.

When the missionary, C.F. Andrews, witnessed the peaceful composure of the Sikh volunteers ruthlessly beaten by police during the anti-government demonstrations at Guru-ka-Bagh in 1923, their Christ-like appearance stirred a deep resonance in his dedicated Christian heart. He afterwards told the Governor of Punjab, "I have seen hundreds of Christs being crucified at Guru-ka-Bagh."[10]

Sikh history is richly adorned with the long hair and beards of its devotees. The illustrations of the royal court of Maharaja Ranjit Singh depict each member with a freely flowing beard. Among men of the Khalsa, the beard has always been a powerful distinguishing characteristic. It is a tradition passed on from the time of Guru Nanak. The face of Guru Khalsa Ji conveys the timeless appearance of saintliness, the human being decorated by God.

In the Punjabi language, there are phrases that reflect the perceived relationship between a man's honour and his beard. To pull a man's beard out (*darhee khonee*) means to disgrace him. One can also speak of the honour or modesty of a man's beard (*darhee dee laaj*) when one wishes to make reference to their respectability.[11]

In Mughal times, tyrant rulers had taken harsh measures to disfigure the holy face of Khalsa. In 1711, Emperor Bahadur Shah had issued a decree:

calling upon all Hindus in the royal camp to shave off their beards. The hair and beard were considered to be the only visible distinction between the two (Sikhs and Hindus), for Sikhs… Would under no circumstances, ever under pain of death, cut or shave their beards or whiskers, or any hair whatever of their body.[12]

Later, another royal order commanded:

"that no non-Moslem should be allowed to have a long beard, and that whosoever was so found, his beard should be pulled out". So this was proclaimed in the imperial territories. In the imperial camp it took such a turn that giant-like commanders of armies went about the bazaars and streets, accompanied by barbers with filthy water in dirty basins. And whomsoever they found, they shaved off his beard with indignity, and pulled his beard and garments. Royal princes, mutsiddis, and other well-known Hindus shaved their beards in their own houses before they came into the royal presence.[13]

Like the Mughals before them, the British who annexed Punjab in 1849 C.E. had little sympathy for the honour and traditions of the Khalsa. In their new territory, the British administrators, saw the possibility of acquiring a mercenary, nominally Sikh, army and – they hoped – a governable and reasonably untroublesome citizenry. Therefore, it should have come as no surprise when the new authorities demanded that all male Sikhs in the employ of the army and civil service take their beards and stuff them out of sight, under their chins, using a beard net.

The net or "jalee" might for a time have served some arguable utilitarian purpose in the army. The munitions in use at the time might well have been considered a fire hazard to a loosely flowing beard. Yet, the dubious advantage to Sikh clerks and other officials of crimping their beards each morning, and the continued use of the jalee in the army long after the safety of the firearms that were used had been much improved, left open to question the real intent behind the prohibition of the open beard.[iii]

Gradually, however, all Sikh men who desired some sort of intercourse with the British took up the daily practice of rolling their beards under their chins. Even proud maharajas, who found their status increasingly tentative under the angrezee raj, began to keep their regal beards discretely tucked under their chins. Symbolically, wearing the beard net was a personal submission to the new masters of the land. It said to the British, "You don't need to be afraid of me. I will work for you. I will eat with you. I can drink with you. I am not a fanatic. I am a moderate Sikh."

Many men began to keep their beards tied up even on off days, at home and at the Gurudwara. They came to consider the jalee a mark of social distinction, a status symbol, a sign of imperial favour. They felt they looked very smart and fashionable with their beards all crimped up. Those Khalsa who were less concerned with "looking smart" and mindful instead of the lack of wisdom in tying one's beard, wore their beards openly, even defiantly. Yet, the practice eventually became so ingrained that, even among Sikhs who dedicated their lives to untying the knot of colonial bondage, there were those who insisted on subjecting themselves each morning to the ordeal of the jalee.

Below is a list of some of the brave saints, martyrs, freedom fighters, and servants of Truth who kept their faces unconstrained by the imperial jalee. Many of their faces adorn the gallery of the Sikh Museum, Amritsar. God knows them all by name.[14]

Sant Baba Attar Singh Ji
Sant Bikram Singh Ji Bedi
Raja Chattar Singh Ji Attariwalla
Giani Dit Singh Ji
Giani Gurmukh Singh Ji Musafir
Sant Baba Isher Singh Ji
Bhai Jodh Singh Ji
Bhai Kahn Singh Ji Nabha
Bhai Kartar Singh Ji Jhabbar
Baba Kharak Singh Ji
Baba Maharaj Singh Ji
Sant Baba Nand Singh Ji
Professor Puran Singh Ji
Baba Ram Singh Ji Namdhari
Bhai Ram Singh Ji
Bhai Sahib Randhir Singh Ji
Maharaja Ripudaman Singh Ji Nabha
Professor Sahib Singh Ji
Sardar Sobha Singh Ji
Master Tara Singh Ji
Sant Teja Singh Ji
Jathedar Teja Singh Ji Akarpuri
Jathedar Teja Singh Ji Bhuchar
Shaheed Teja Singh Ji Samundri
Sardar Thakur Singh Ji Sandawalia
Jathedar Udham Singh Ji Nagoke
Bhai Vir Singh Ji

Around the end of the 19th century, a new quirk of fashion came into vogue in British society. Up until that time, many Englishmen had kept prominent beards, or sideburns and mustaches. In much earlier times, the Celtic forebears of the modern Englishman had kept their hair intact. But now, the style became to reduce what hirsute vestiges of manhood remained or to shave them off entirely.

The British called those who adopted the practice "clean-shaven". The term contained a certain bias in favour of keeping one's face beardless. The unspoken presumption of anyone who used the terms "clean-shaven" and "nonclean-shaven" was that shaving the hair off a person's face made it "clean". The natural corollary was that an unshaven face was unhygienic.

This ingrained etymological bias served well the prejudice of those times. The term "clean-shaven" was coined by the American poet Longfellow, around 1863.[15] The Spirit of Khalsa, however, would have been better served by the original descriptive term in English, which dated its usage back to the time of its greatest bard, William Shakespeare. To him, a beardless man was "bare-faced". By implication, a man who had disowned his beard was shameless and without principles.[16]

Plate 7 Guru Nanak, his holy successors and his disciples, Bhai Bala and Bhai Mardana. All of the Guru's and their

most devoted disciples were fully-bearded, except for Guru Harkrishan (8th Guru), who passed from this Earth at the young age of eight years. Guru Ram Das (4th Guru) is known for his very long beard, with which he is said to have wiped the dust from the feet of a distinguished guest, Baba Siri Chand, the elder son of Guru Nanak.

Plate 8   "The Creation of Adam" by Michelangelo (1475-1564)

Plate 9 "God Judging Adam" by
William Blake (1757-1827)

III - DRESSING FOR IMPERIALISM

Guru Gobind Singh Ji -

So long as the Khalsa remains distinct, I will render it all glory.

• • • • • • •

Like every conquering, colonizing people, 19th century Britons not only brought their cultural baggage and assumptions along with them: they wore them. The angrezees were recognizable at a distance by their hats and shoes and the particular European cut of their clothing. Much of what they wore, especially the fashions of the British women, followed trends dictated by the whims and extravagances of designers and courtiers "on the continent". What the Europeans wore was not always practical – taking for example the hat and tie of the English gentleman, or the exaggerated proportions and elaborate underpinnings of a Victorian lady's garments – but they did achieve one thing. They set the governing race apart. The costumes of the British gave them the feeling that they were distinguished.

The indigenous Punjabi family, for its part, wore the attire to which it had been accustomed. The loose, flowing comfortable clothing were well-suited to the climate and local culture. The sardar was outfitted in turban, "kurta", and "pyjama" or "chadar", while the sardardi wore "chuni", "kameez" and "salwaar". All these were readily made from cottons, silks and wools available locally. Since this attire did not derive its inspiration from any "avant garde" situation outside Punjab, this style of dressing retained it fashionability and usefulness over many centuries.

In time, European-style clothing also came to be tailored and manufactured in India to serve the needs of the British. Those native Indians who wished to identify, and be identified, with the ruling class also took up the Englishman's style of dress. It is significant that relatively few women took up the Western look. (i) By and large, only the men, the bread-earners of the traditional Sikh households, adopted the ferenghee dress with a view to enhancing their status in colonial society. Yet every attempt at imitating the physical appearance of the "goras" was doomed and determined from its outset. Simply put, native Indians were visibly and demonstrably not Europeans.

Since the early 1860's, the Namdhari Sikhs, taking their inspiration from Baba Ram Singh, opposed both style and substance of the Englishman's fashion industry.[17] They resisted the economics of buying British-spun fabric, when cotton could more easily and cheaply be spun at home. Instead of Western-style three-piece suits and dresses, they wore the traditional Punjabi attire made from hand-woven cotton fabric, known as "khaddar".[18]

The S.G.P.C., along with the Congress Party of Mohandas Karamchand "Mahatma" Gandhi, joined the Namdharis in 1921 C.E. in encouraging the home manufacture of khaddar. They also expanded the scope of the Namdhari boycott to include all foreign goods, including fashions. Wearing clothes made of khaddar became a popular form of resistance to foreign domination.[19]

After the massacre of Sikhs at Nanakana Sahib on February 20 1921 C.E., black-dyed fabric came to have a special significance. The Akali Dal called on everyone to wear black as a protest against the government's oppressive policies. Turbans and chunis were blackened at night, when the watchful eyes of the angrezees and their collaborators could not detect the effluence of the dying vats. Sikhs wearing black were liable to be harassed and persecuted in every possible way. Many who performed government service were summarily dismissed. In spite of the government's attempts to intimidate them, tens of thousands of heroes and martyrs came out to confront the British regime in black-dyed, home-spun defiance.[20]

Plate 10 Khalsa couple wearing the Guru's Bana

Plate 11   Bhangra dancing in festive Punjabi attire

Plate 12 English couple wearing fashionable Victorian attire of 1859. (Wikipedia: 1850's in Western Fashion   [accessed 08-01-21])

Plate 13   Edwin Samuel Montagu, British Secretary of State (1917-1922), with an associate in fashionable top hat and tails. (Wikipedia: Edwin Samuel Montagu [accessed 30/12/20])

IV – HER MAJESTY'S PURVEYORS OF NARCOTICS

From the Hymns in Praise of Guru Ram Das Ji –

We are full of shortcomings and without a single merit. Abandoning Nectar, we eat poison.

● ● ● ● ● ● ●

A few years' perspective can be a remarkable thing. A century ago, the pandits of European imperialism made much of the "white man's burden", the perceived mission of "higher cultures" – meaning Western, Caucasian – to exert the influence of their supposedly superior commerce, science, and religion on the rest of the world. Now, we can see that the greater part of that alleged burden likely stemmed from a troubled conscience.

When English adventurers first came to the fabled land of maharajas, they found themselves at a distinct disadvantage. While they wished to return home with their cargo holds filled with India's exotic spices, finely-woven fabrics, handcrafted and precious jewelry, they had nothing of any value to trade. The people of India did not need British woolens, and other industries in Britain were not yet technically advanced. The English found the only way they could buy Indian goods was with silver they might earn selling African slaves to the Spanish in America and the West Indies.[21]

Eventually, those traders-cum-adventurers established their base in Bengal. There, they used their position of military and political dominance to *"weigh the balance of exchange and secure the maximum goods for the minimum payment... The European mercantile bourgeoisie never drew a sharp line between trade and plunder; the original Merchant Adventurers of England often combined trade with piracy. Now, whatever margin there had been between trade and plunder began to grow conspicuously thin."*[22] Inspired with imperial arrogance and rapacity, the English virtually enslaved the guilds of highly-skilled weavers, who were rounded up and forced to work for next to nothing, and established indigo plantations, where the labouring conditions were cruel and dehumanizing.(i)

Encouraged by the profitability of their operations in Bengal, the angrezees hoped to extend their sphere of trade into the Far East. Once they entered China, however, they ran into the same difficulty they had first experienced in India. Other than silver, they possessed nothing of any value to the Chinese. However, the British were quick to recognize and capitalize on a craving among the oriental leisure class for opium from abroad.

The scourge of opium addition, which within 150 years had penetrated and corrupted all classes of Chinese society, originated in the company of certain idle and wealthy young men of Formosa, who in 1620 C.E. developed a taste for smoking a mixture of opium and tobacco from England's American colonies.[23] The traders exploited this weakness. By 1773, the British East India Company took over from the Portuguese the dubious distinction of being China's number one purveyor of imported opium. Before long, they had established a complete monopoly from the cultivation of the seedling in Malwa (Punjab) and Bihar to the sale of the finished product by auction in Bengal. Thus, a profitable balance of trade was established: British opium, grown in Indian or imported from Turkey, for Chinese tea and silk. To those who opposed Britain's open involvement in the burgeoning narcotics trade, the Duke of Wellington replied in March of 1836 C.E. that his government not only refused to frown on the traffic in opium, but cherished it, extended it, and promoted it![24]

The role of British traders as traffickers in addictive and mind-altering substances cannot be fully appreciated unless one recognizes that the English national beverage itself has habit-forming and mildly psychotropic properties. Tea was first introduced in 1657 C.E. at one of London's then existing two thousand coffee houses. The English had already been habitual coffee drinkers for some time. Cleverly merchandised as *"That Excellent and by all Physicians approved Chinese drink,"* tea eventually surpassed coffee in popularity.[25]

Anyone who has acquired a taste for coffee or tea is aware of their stimulative physical and psychological properties. The active ingredient of both beverages is caffeine ($C_6H_{10}N_4O_6\text{-}H_2O$). In small dosages, this drug can induce wakefulness and quickening of the heart and breath. Taken in large amounts, it has been observed to cause restlessness, insomnia, convulsions, even physical collapse.[26]

Although personal tolerance levels vary, heavy drinkers of tea or coffee are commonly seen to suffer from hypertension and some forms of chronic anxiety.(ii) Like any other kind of addict, someone who is habituated to caffeine performs at a less than optimal level unless their metabolism is aroused by their drug of choice. In ordinary language, the regular drinkers of tea or coffee does not feel fully awake and is unable to cope effectively with the demands of the day until they have their morning beverage.

The British colonial government began plans for large-scale tea cultivation in India in 1834 C.E.[27] Thereafter, it's "civilizing influence" came to be felt everywhere the English exerted their ubiquitous presence. Free packets of tea were distributed from door to door in a campaign directed at urban Indian households. In the early years of this century, zealous merchants were known to penetrate the vast Punjabi hinterland in trucks loaded with a gramophone and large urns of steaming "chaee", serenading the lassi-drinking rural communities and impressing them with their exotic, modern brew.(iii)

From the 17th to the early 20th century C.E., English traders were the world's drug dealers par excellence. They plied their highly addictive tobacco products from America to the peoples of the world. They monopolized the supply of opium to China, and humiliated the Chinese in two crushing "opium wars". Through its tea monopoly, the East India Company then habituated the people of the British Empire and beyond to a lifestyle dependent on Chinese, then Indian and Sri Lankan, teas. And throughout that far-flung empire, in its mess halls and clubs, taverns, inns and trading posts, the pernicious British firewater flowed freely, or not so freely, to inebriate and disorient just about everyone.

The Sikh response to this intoxicating onslaught was not altogether resolute. While Sikhs had not generally been known as users of tobacco and opiates, the otherwise ultra-orthodox Nihangs had cherished their so-called "amrit", a cannabis-based, psychedelic elixir. Sikh men had also been widely known as notorious boozers well before the arrival of British rum and whiskey. Ranjit Singh, the maharaja who so lionized the Punjab, was himself an infamous imbiber of debilitating spirits. Once the English took over the government of Punjab, they condoned, encouraged, and profited from the alcohol trade. Those Punjabis so privileged as to gain access, by favour or service, to the sequestered realms of colonial high society, saw for themselves these supposed purveyors of "higher culture" in the intoxicated atmosphere of their social and semi-official functions.

The Namdharis and other devout Sikhs did raise their voices against the scourge of alcoholism. In 1921 C.E., the S.G.P.C. also issued a belated call to boycott British-made spirits.[28] The

S.G.P.C. call may have been based more on political than moral considerations, however, since most of the liquor consumed by Sikhs was home-made. The best that can be said in this light is that Sikh women remained virtually untouched by the blight of alcoholism. A Sikh woman alcoholic was virtually unknown.

However, both women and men of Punjab turned into great consumers of tea during the British period. The caffeine-based beverage had none of the moral stigma of alcohol, tobacco or opiates attached to it. To those who confessed to the superiority of British moral and societal values, the rituals of taking "high tea" or "having someone over for tea" even seemed to have some inherently uplifting spiritual characteristics, not unlike the penchant of the Japanese for tea ceremonies.

This colonial brew came to be an indispensable part of the langar in virtually every Gurudwara. Soon tens, even hundreds, of thousands of Sikhs had acquired the habit of downing a cup of their drug of choice before starting their morning prayers. For them, this chaee of the angrezees, like Amrit of the Nihangs, came to acquire a virtually religious significance.

BADGES OF BONDAGE

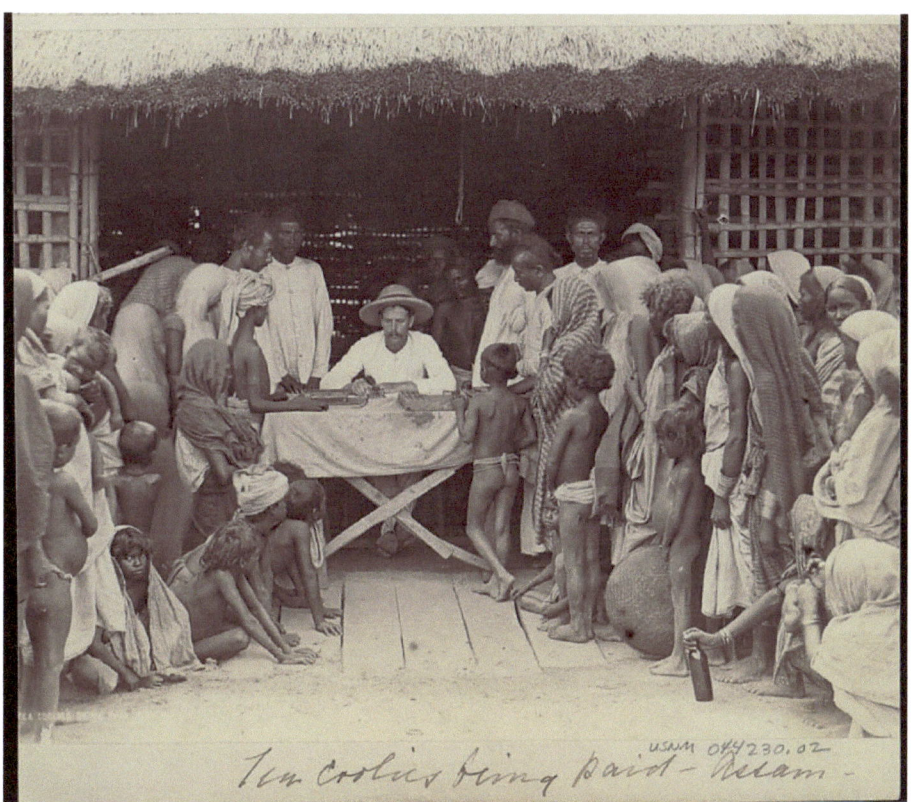

Plate 14 Assamese tea plantation workers being paid by Englishman. While industrial scale tea production began in the mid-1800's, the marketing of tea in India did not begin until the early 1900's. (Wikipedia: Indian Tea Culture [16/01/21])

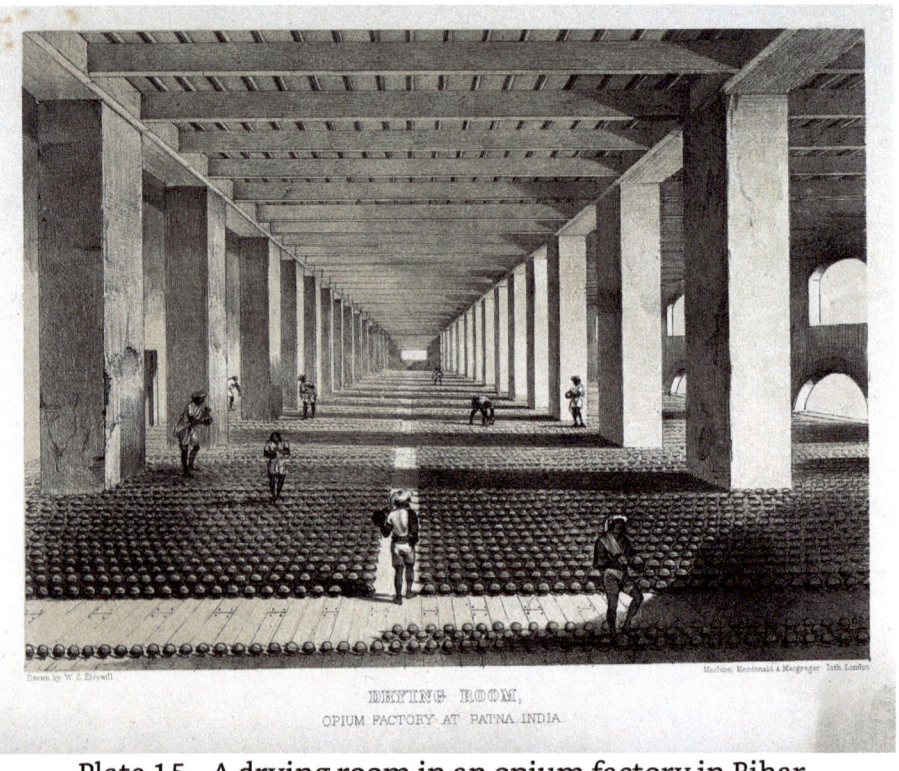

Plate 15   A drying room in an opium factory in Bihar. Chinese opium consumption increased exponentially during the 1800's much of it grown in India. (Wikipedia: History of Opium in China [accessed 16/01/21])

V – THE JOBS OF THE ENGLISH

Guru Nanak Dev Ji -

Out of Your Divine Nature,
Comes seeing and hearing.
Out of Your Divine Nature,
We experience dread and the essence of happiness.
Because of Your Divine Nature,
There are dark underworlds beneath
And sublime heavens above.
Through Your Divine Nature,
The entire creation is sustained.

• • • • • • •

    To take the psyche of the Sikh people and remold it to serve the interests of their colonial masters might be considered a matter of education. The British governor-general spoke openly in those terms. This process of education, however, involved more than simply training Sikhs to speak and understand English.[i] It was also more than a matter of teaching the Sikh people to think like Europeans. What was needed, as Lord Dalhousie must have realized, was to bring the Sikh nation over to an entirely different way of being.

While the British valued the self-reliance and productivity they found in the rural-based Punjabi economy, the government's overall strategy lay in harnessing every one of the countless individual "units of production" in the vast Indian subcontinent to the larger needs of the imperial economy. There was a pressure to enhance efficiency and think in terms of global economy. According to the 19th century C.E. model, enhanced productivity meant larger production units: bigger farms, larger plantations, more gigantic factories. Bigger farms needed increased irrigation, more water, new canals. The empire's plantations and factories required workers who would work together, speak one language, and willingly accept employment, transfer, and dismissal according to the impersonal dictates of imperial supply and demand. Plantations and factories needed roadways and railways in order to receive raw materials, labourers and machinery, then ship their produce as quickly as possible to the market that commanded the highest price.

The schemes of the Englishman had little tolerance for what might appear to him as an incomprehensible quagmire of pagan prejudices and superstitions. His orders were to "rationalize, centralize and modernize". In the pursuit of these objectives, colonial officials forged ahead, sometimes regardless of time-honoured traditions and religious sensitivities. The agents of British colonialism dedicated themselves to the objective of weaving from the subcontinent's many-hued strands of race, culture, caste, and religion, one single unified cloth - commercially viable, religiously inert, and submissive to the wants of the sovereign British power invested at Westminster Abbey.

Imperial language, a novel vocabulary encompassing new technologies and administrative systems, penetrated and sometimes subverted local ways of speaking. The *lambardars* situated in every village, responsible for taxation, became *numberdars,* literally "number people."

Innovations from abroad might be shortened or kept, with a Punjabi inflection. "Railway train" was shortened to *rail*, "photograph" turned to *foto*, and "congress" became a political party with reach across Hindustan. But spunky Punjabis were capable to coining their own terms, as in the case of *putleeghar*, literally a "puppet house," which is what they called a textile mill, for it was clear to all concerned that while the workers manufactured cloth on an unprecedented scale, the process was intensely dehumanizing, rendering adult human beings into mere puppets for the bosses above them.

Even as English society was becoming increasingly secularized, and the role of its church as chief moral authority, educator and custodian of social welfare was eroded, the Sikhs of far-off Punjab were asked to give up a rich system of beliefs, customs and values which informed the very essence of their identity. They were asked, indirectly, to give up their belief in living saints. The skeptical English did not allow of any. Their saints had all been decided by the Pope of Rome some centuries before. The British were made very uneasy by the movements of outspoken Sikh holy men, such as Baba Maharaj Singh and Baba Ram Singh, who gathered large followings wherever they went.(ii)

The Sikhs, who lived by a daily regimen of religious observances, and considered certain times and places as especially sacred and important, were asked to adopt a secular system of belief in which nothing was particularly sacred and everything was equally insignificant.

The Sikhs, who considered the human body to be the temporary dwelling of the One Eternal Being, and recognized miracles, and the healing power of the sight of a saint, and the sound of sacred Gurubani, were asked to accept the perspective which had overtaken Europe, that consciousness was merely an outcome of certain material conditions, and therefore a doctor of the mind was first a physician of the physical body.

The Sikhs, who embodied an elaborate and accommodating social structure which attached a great deal of significance to social distinctions and the honour of one's family, clan and community, were asked to give all this up for an impersonal money-based system in which an individual was just an interchangeable cog on a vast wheel of global production and consumption, where honour was considered to be a quaint and slightly ridiculous notion, and all that really mattered was what one owned and what one did for money.(iii)

The men who left the British Isles to administer the Punjab had long ago given up honouring their river spirits. Generations ago, they had lost their ties of clan and lineage. They had come to Punjab inspired by neither tradition nor honour. They simply had a job to do.

Plate 16 Photograph of the first train on the rail line from Sialkot, Punjab to Jammu, 1890 (Wikipedia: Jammu-Sialkot Line [accessed: 16/01/21])

Plate 17   The opening of the Sirhind canal at Rupar in 1882 (British Library [accessed: 16/01/21])

Plate 18   Men of the Sikh Regiment in China, circa 1860. Punjabi Sikhs were recruited as brave and loyal subjects and members of a "martial race." (Wikipedia: Sikh Regiment Martial Race [accessed 16/01/21])

Plate 19   A Postcard showing Sikh soldiers on their arrival in France In 1914 at the outset of the First World War

VI – COLONIAL JUSTICE

Guru Nanak Dev Ji -

*This Dark Age is a knife and the kings are butchers.
Justice has taken wings and flown away.*

• • • • • • •

By the time the British took over the government of Punjab, the people of the region already had well-established traditions of justice. The most common forum for settling disputes was the panchayat. It consisted of a council of the five most respected members of a community. Hindus, Moslems and Sikhs all used panchayats. It was an old and honoured system. There was a saying, "God lives in the panchayat". (*Panchan main Parmayshar hai.*)[29] Among Sikhs, a gathering of five Khalsa was especially respected because of the Tenth Master's dictate that there is no distinction between such a "Punj" and himself.

These councils of five worked so well that even some members of British's colonial administration praised it. Sir George Campbell, a deputy commissioner of east Punjab in the early 1840's C.E., remarked:

"Certainly my experience of the village institutions on the Sutlej, where perhaps they are at their best, made me appreciate them very much indeed, and I think they are not only good for India, but for some other countries as well. In fact, I can deliberately say that far from

imposing my ideas on these people, it was from them that I learned ideas of local self-government which I retain to this day, and which I have brought with me to my native country."[30]

Malcolm, the British historian, approvingly quoted a Sikh who had settled in Calcutta, who spoke of the panchayat system's "great superiority over the vexatious legal system of the English Government, which was tedious, vexatious and expensive, and advantageous only to clever rogues."[31]

Regardless, the colonial government set about importing British notions of justice. According to them, justice needed to be centrally administered, it needed a written legal code, and that code needed to be uniformly enforced throughout their domain.

The British altogether ignored and circumvented the panchayats. The indigenous pride and spirit of local self-reliance which they represented ran contrary to the entire imperial ethic. The angrezees established their own courts, which carried the authoritative stamp of the Englishman's empire, throughout the Punjab. As a consequence, many cases which had earlier been decided by the panchayats, began to be brought before the British courts, either in the first instance or on appeal.[32]

The English also did not favour the idea of separate courts for Hindus and Moslems. Under Sikh rule, members of Punjab's largest religious communities could choose to be tried according to their own sacred traditions.[33] The British discouraged this practice.[34]

As a result, people in communities throughout Punjab, even those with strong religious convictions, publicly began to allow their colonial masters to decide fundamental questions of right and wrong for them. The appropriation of the dispensation of public justice was an important psychological victory for the British.

Not everyone, however, surrendered their right of self-jurisprudence to the angrezees. Since the 1860's C.E., the Namdharis had earned the government's displeasure by settling their differences within their community.[35] In 1921 C.E., the S.G.P.C. also rejected the colonial justice system and issued a call for Sikhs to return to the traditional system of panchayat.[36]

Plate 20   Courthouse in Gujranwala in 1865

Plate 21 Amritsar Town Hall, built in 1866

Plate 22 The execution of 65 Namdhari Sikhs in 1872. (Wikipedia: Blowing from a Gun [accessed 16/01/21])

BADGES OF BONDAGE

Plate 23 Lahore High Court in the 1880's

VII – A BRITISH EDUCATION

Guru Nanak Dev Ji -

Those who are learned, dedicate themselves to the good of all. Controlling their bestial inclinations, they make their home a holy place of pilgrimage.

• • • • • • •

The main weapon of the British, by which they hoped over time to subjugate the independent spirit of Khalsa, was its system of so-called "education". On five continents, wherever the British established colonies, missions, and ports of call, they saw to it that schools were set up to mold new generations of loyal colonials. As it happened, the desire of the administration to educate the youth of the Sikhs coincided with a desire among Sikh, Hindu and, to a lesser extent, Moslem parents in Punjab to see their children educated by the English.

It is striking to note the place of education in Punjab society during the time of Maharaja Ranjeet Singh. In his book, *History of Indigenous Education in Punjab,* published in 1882, education scholar and founder of Government College at Lahore founder, G. W. Leitner asserted that the Punjab was better off in the days of the maharaja than under the British. Maharaja Ranjeet Singh collected more in revenue in his last years than the colonizers and spent a greater percentage of the state's income on education.[37]

Leitner chronicled the decline of a number of important schools in Amritsar and elsewhere under the British East India Company, then under the Raj.[38]

Pakistani scholar, Robina Shoeb recently brought to light an effective device for literacy in Punjab that reflected Maharaja Ranjeet Singh's keenness that his people learn to read and write. "Quaida Noor" was designed by his minister, Fakir Nuruddin and proved very effective in teaching literacy and basic math skills. Originally, 5,000 copies were made and distributed to village *lambardars* throughout his domain. The *lambardars* were to master the Quaida Noor in three months, then make and distribute five copies to five more people in their village. They were also required to write a letter to the maharaja stating they had learned the Quaida Noor and distributed five copies in their community. Maharaja kept discipline by dismissing *lambardars* who did not write him.[39]

1849 C.E. saw the establishment of the first British government-sponsored school in Amritsar. Thereafter, except for a lull during the uprising of 1857 C.E., the building of new schools and training of teachers went ahead at a dizzying pace. By 1901 C.E., there were 2833 primary and 351 secondary schools, plus 15 colleges and a university in the British province. In 1919 C.E., the government took the further measure of making primary school compulsory for all boys.[40]

The curriculum of these British-inspired schools differed a great deal from the Punjabi madrasas that had gone before them. The main subjects in the new schools were grammar and arithmetic, and the history and geography of the British Empire. Religion, which had been the mainstay of the previous systems of Indian education, was not taught except in the Christian schools.

Urdu, which the English had made the official language of Punjab, was the basic medium of instruction. English was taught at the larger schools. Hindi and Arabic were not considered useful, and therefore never entered into the curriculum. In 1859 C.E., Sanskrit and Gurmukhi were dropped from the curriculum of the original Amritsar school. Thereafter, these sacred languages and Persian could only be studied at the higher levels of education.[41]

European-style teaching also differed from the indigenous systems in its overall approach:

Indian education... was personal and based on the family system... The characteristic spirit of Indian education (is that it) is a personal discipleship of the pupil to the teacher, and religion is inseparable from this discipleship... Education was considered a personal and family-like process: the teacher had to live with his pupils, talking and listening to them, encouraging and praising, scolding and punishing them. And since earning a living had not yet become the primary goal of education, this possibly less business-like, but certain more scientific, attitude was followed unmolested.[42]

In contrast with the Indian tradition of learning, the British colonial arrangement was both irreligious and personally alienating. The fundamental questions of a young person's relationship to their Creator, moral living, and spiritual well-being were deliberately overlooked (except in the Christian schools). The natural bond between teacher and student became secondary to the relationship of each of them to the school, the institution of education. The student-teacher relationship, which had been lifelong and profound, became short-lived and increasingly casual. Teachers were assigned to specific age groups, and limited to certain subjects. While under the traditional madrasa system, groups of six students had been typical,[43] several times that many were commonly crowded together under the new arrangement. Moreover, teachers were routinely transferred, promoted, and pensioned off at the pleasure of the bureaucracy that ran the system, thereby ensuring the complete alienation of the students and teachers alike.

Essentially, the English schools were factories of cultural

assimilation. Their raw material was the innocent children of the Sikh nation. Each morning, they assembled in classrooms throughout Punjab to be taught some worldly skills that might make them useful to the angrezee raj, and to be fed the poison that their culture was inferior in every way to that of the clever Europeans. Then, as in any other factory, at a predetermined hour, everyone returned home, the business of "education" being done for another day.

There are not many statistics available to us that might help us measure the extent to which the British were successful in their effort to indoctrinate the rising Sikh generations with their ideology and lifestyle. How many took up the English style of dress, or cut their hair, or neglected their daily prayers as a result of the angrezee schooling system is difficult to say. However, one statistic survives. From 1881 to 1931 C.E., the number of Christians in Punjab rose from less than 2,000 to an astonishing 400,000.[44]

While the mainstream of Sikhs did not object, but rather welcomed the opportunities for material advancement afforded by the British schools, the Namdharis did object:

The Namdharis were not opposed to education as such, for the greatest stress was laid by Baba Ram Singh on the teaching of the mother tongue, Punjabi, through its own script, and on the imparting of religious instruction. What they were opposed to was the new system of education introduced by the foreign rulers. They disliked it for its materialistic approach and content, and thought nothing but evil could result from it. That is why all educational institutions modeled on Western lines, whether run by the Government or privately, were avoided.[45]

The struggle for the minds and hearts of the children of the Sikh nation during the period of British colonial domination saw some peculiar developments. One of them was anticipated by an astute officer of the East India Company when the issue of providing English education to the people of Bengal was discussed, around 1795 C.E.;

> "If English language, if English opinions and improvements are introduced in our Asiatic possessions... will not the people learn to desire English liberty and the English form of government...? Will not the people think it a hardship to be subject, and pay tribute, to a foreign country? And finally, will they not cast off that subjugation and assert their independence?"[46]

By the late 19th century C.E., a prominent Sikh movement, called the "Singh Sabha", had arisen. The members of the movement determined the Sikh nation needed an educational system on the British model, that it could call their own. The members of the Singh Sabha included a number of men who were thought to be among the leading Sikh thinkers of that time. While they organized themselves along Western parliamentary lines, they considered their prime mission to be the preservation of Sikh identity.[47]

With the support of the Government and a number of Sikh maharajas, the Singh Sabha was able to open an institution of higher learning in Amritsar in 1892 C.E. The extraordinary redstone structure was named Khalsa College.

Within a few years, however matters became out of hand as the college became a hotbed of anti-colonial sentiment. Finally, in 1907 C.E., the Government felt compelled to put an end to the "unhealthy atmosphere" at Khalsa College. By revising the constitution of the institution's managing committee, the British managed to take full control of the college from the Sikhs. A number of teachers were dismissed. The Secretary and highest Sikh office-holder, Sunder Singh Majithia, resigned in protest.[48]

BADGES OF BONDAGE

Plate 24   Church in Murree, at the edge of the Himalayas, in 1860

Plate 25   A government school in Amritsar in 1870. The British moved quickly to create institutions in Punjab to bend the minds of the young to their liking. The Wards School was established in 1868 at the British cantonment in Ambala for the education of young princes of Punjab. Moved to Lahore in 1886, it was renamed "the Punjab's Chief's College," then "Aitchison College," and remained focused on Westernizing the sons of the ruling families, encouraging social conformity and instilling an unquestioning admiration for the British Empire. (Grewal & Banga [2018], Wikipedia: Aitchison College [accessed 08/01/21])

Plate 26   Khalsa College, Amritsar, founded 1892

VIII – CONCLUSION: "ANGREZEEMAT"

Guru Gobind Singh Ji -

"I do not care for one who only calls himself my Sikh. Rather, I love the abiding intelligence and honour of one who lives as a Sikh!"

• • • • • • •

Governance is never a relationship of equals, yet neither can it be engaged in without some implicit understanding. There are always some on either side of the divide with a degree of appreciation of the ways and values of the other.

Being an unequal relationship, Sikh and Indian values and beliefs did not penetrate British ways of thinking and behaving to nearly the extent that "angrezeemat," the English way of being, entered and came to dominate many aspects of Punjabi life. Except the discovery of an exotic new setting for English novels and poesy, the adaptation of some Indian architectural motifs, the advent of a few vegetarian restaurants in London, and the philosophical excursions of the theosophists, the ordinary English way of life remained hardly affected. While the resolute conquerors from overseas pillaged India's treasure-houses and trammeled her pleasure gardens, their hearts largely remained unmoved, and essentially English.

The fall of the Sikh kingdom and arrival of angrezee raj

shook the belief of many Punjabis in their customary way of life. Especially in the urban centres, and particularly among those Sikhs who ventured outside of Punjab, but even in the fertile Punjabi countryside, new English ways of looking, thinking, speaking, and behaving exerted a ubiquitous influence.(i)

The defeat of the Khalsa army augured the arrival of a strange new era in the domain which was home to the spirit of Guru Nanak. When Sikhs swore allegiance "to God and the Queen", they found they had pledged themselves to a foreign god and an alien monarch.

Through their schooling and through their employment practices, in what they encouraged and what they condoned, the smart British colonials fostered a different kind of Sikh from what his forefathers had known. He lived by English standards of justice and accepted the conventions of English social mores and graces. His outlook was essentially secular and democratic. He was socially homogenous and monogamous. He dressed and often spoke like an Englishman. His home was furnished with a chesterfield and a coffee table and a European bed. Its walls were adorned with pieces of English motifs. At dinnertime, he sat at a table and chair and ate from English China using English silverware, knives and forks and spoons. He was a tea drinker and – as they would say – if he occasionally ate the meat or smoked the odd cigarette or drank the spirits of the English, "who was there to know or care?"

Plate 27 Festive Punjabi food: saag, makki roti, raita, slice of onion, hot green pepper

Plate 28   Traditional English Sunday lunch: roast beef, roast potatoes, vegetables, Yorkshire pudding

Plate 29   Jallianwala Bagh memorial, Amritsar, memorializing the massacre of hundreds of citizens gathered in the park on April 13, 1919 by Colonel Reginald Dyer

Plate 30 Boy and dog in the Bengal famine of 1943. An estimated two million people died largely as a result of government war policies that restricted people's access to rice. (Wikipedia: Bengal famine of 1943 [accessed 31/12/20])

Plate 31   Emergency trains crowded with desperate refugees during the partition of Pakistan and India in 1947. At least half a million people died and 12 million were made homeless in the violence and chaos. (Wikipedia: Partition of India [accessed 31/12/20])

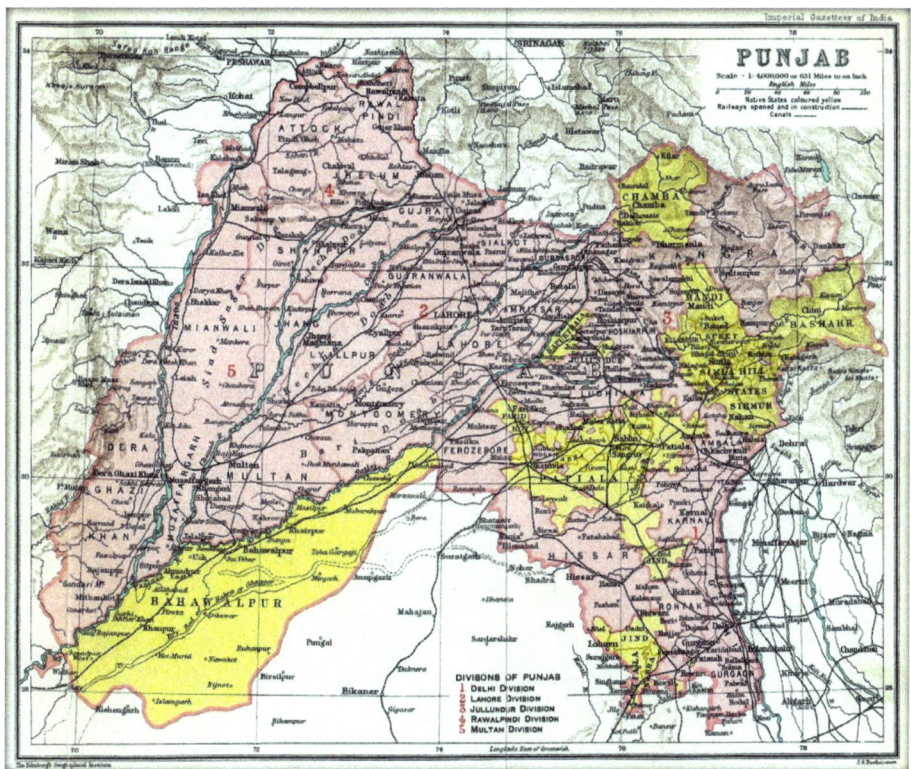

Plate 32   1909 government map of Punjab showing new railways and canals

EPILOGUE

Guru Arjun Dev Ji -

O Savior Lord, save us and carry us across. Uplift
us and give us the excellence.
You have given us the touch of the Guru's Lotus Feet
and our works are embellished with perfection.
You have become Merciful, Kind and Compassionate.
Our minds do not forget You.
In the companionship of those who apply your sacred discipline,
You save us from misfortune, slander and disaster.
In an instant, you finish off the godless, slanderous enemies.

• • • • • • •

It is an educated understanding that the trader-adventurers of Britain brought even the great empires of Asia to their knees because of the blessings bestowed on them by their industrial revolution. Better science forged superior armaments and more efficient technologies of manufacture, transport, and communication. The industrial revolution also led to superior organization and use of manpower, while the fruits of the revolution gave Europeans an uncommon spirit of self-confidence and enterprise.[49]

The first half of the 19th century of the Christian era saw the expansion of Khalsa Raj, even as the British empire extended its influence. Yet, it was not the same Khalsa that had rallied around the standard of Guru Gobind Singh, and enjoyed brief sovereignty under Banda Sigh Bahadur. For more than one hundred years (1699-1801 C.E.) the Khalsa managed to hold its own on a precarious frontier against genocidal tyrants and massive plundering armies. However, during the later years of Maharaja Ranjit Singh's rule (1801-1839 C.E.), the ascetic spirit and bond of unity succumbed to an era of drunken living and brazen self-interest. Given that the Maharaja had not made any arrangements for succession to his throne, all hell, predictably, broke loose when he was no more.

Just as Guru Nanak Dev Ji had been a master at inspiring unity among peoples of diverse backgrounds and religions, the British were masters of divide and rule. Even as Guru Nanak had encouraged Hindus and Moslems to live in peace, and even as Maharaja Ranjit Singh had administered a kingdom where Moslems, Hindus and Sikhs increasingly worked together in mutual respect and harmony, in rather the opposite way, the British overran Punjab's religious and administrative tradition, and fostered distinctions and divisions which ultimately did not serve the people.

Many Sikhs opposed the secular, dehumanizing spirit of this colonialism, which in its own way was no less brutal than the holocausts perpetrated by the Mughals. Other Sikhs thought they could play the game of the angrezees to their advantage. Great was their surprise, their shock and dismay, when in 1947 C.E. the price of their complicity was paid in the bifurcation of the very heartland of Guru Nanak, the great messenger of human unity, divinity and faith. The foreigners paid their former subjects handsomely when, after all was said and done, the heartland of the once great empire, where Nanak had inspired people to live together in peace and harmony, was awash in a sea of hatred and human blood.

There is no point in blaming leaders. It is not helpful to heap contempt or scorn. Everyone was doing what they thought was best. Sometimes they simply had no idea what they were doing.

As things stand, the Sikh nation is not truly itself. It has not, as yet, come into its own. It is the scion of a vast legacy, a technology of mind and an aptitude of spirit, but it lacks confidence. Many mornings, the world awakes and seeks the handsome face of the saint soldier who would come from the East and rescue it from its secular nightmare, but that face is not there. It is shaven or made-up or beard-netted or contorted in a thousand ways. For many Sikhs, their self-image bears no resemblance to reality at all, and if they cannot find themselves in their own personal mirror, how is the world to recognize this handsome, heroic Khalsa?

NOTES

(i) The British had tried in 1838 to turn Afghanistan into a dependency. Three years later, they were forced to beat a bloody retreat through the Khyber Pass. There were those in the British government who supported continuing friendly relations with the Sikh raj so long as the formidable military might of the Sikh kingdom of Punjab provided a buffer against the hostile Afghanis and the possibility of invasion from Russia.

The angrezees held the Khalsa army in high regard. It was well known that the army of the Sikh raj had been trained in the modern means of warfare by imported European specialists, and that its discipline and equipment were not to be disparaged. The Sikh gunners' rapidity and accuracy of fire was comparable with that of the French. A British officer who witnessed the siege of Multan (1848-9) paid the Sikh raj's infantry the highest complement possible by saying they charges into battle "like Britons".[50]

When hostilities with the Sikh kingdom did break out, and British army prepared to do battle at Ferozeshah, one could read the grimness with which they anticipated doing battle with the Khalsa army by their gesture of allowing a German officer who had been accompanying them, to take his leave beforehand. The night before battle, the British soldiery busied themselves settling their worldly effects and writing their families, for what many feared might be the last time.

Sir Henry Hardinge, who had only recently been designated Governor-General, did not take the prospect of fighting the Khalsa army lightly. As a veteran of the Napoleonic Wars, he decided to personally join his forces facing the Khalsa army, much to the chagrin of his commander-in-chief, whom he then over-ruled numerous times in the heat of battle. Despite Hardinge's best efforts, and in spite of the traitorous actions of Lal Singh and Tej Singh, on the Sikh side, matters became so desperate for the British at Ferozeshah that preparations were made to destroy all the state papers and to offer an unconditional surrender to the Sikhs.

When the resurgent Khalsa faced British again during the Second Sikh War (1848-9), the imperialist army faced a similar imbroglio at Chillianwala. A British historian stated, *"Chillianwala was not a victory. When news of Chillianwala reached England, the nation was stricken with profound emotion. A long series of military successes had ill-fitted it to hear with composure of British guns and British standards taken and of British cavalry flying before the enemy..."*[51] Bhai Sahib Sirdar Kapur Singh, whose great grandfather had fought at Chillianwala, relates *"that the Sikhs for full twelve hours pursued the scattered British soldiers in all directions, who when overtaken would fall on their knees to beg for mercy, saying 'ham tumhara gai' (I am like a defenceless cow to you) on the sight of a Sikh soldier."*[52]

Introduction

(i) After the martyrdom of Banda Singh Bahadur, many looked to the holy consorts of the founder of the Khalsa, Mata Sundri and Mata Sahib Dewan, for leadership and inspiration. In 1721 C.E., Mata Sundri sent the venerable Bhai Mani Singh from Delhi to be head priest and custodian of the Harimandir Sahib. From that point on, the Khalsa met twice a year in Amritsar.

Mata Sahib Dewan and Mata Sundri remained at their respective residences in Delhi and Mathura. From the number of edicts they issued, it is clear they continued to be active in the affairs of the Khalsa, particularly in the area of finance, the raising and disbursement of funds for the Sikh free kitchens and various other causes.

(ii) During this period, the British were so presumptuous as to instruct their agent in Punjab to *"make clear to the Sikhs that his government would recognize no form of government other than a monarchy."*[53]

Chapter One – The Sikhism of Subservience

(i)   Responding to the general outcry around the massacre at Jallianwala Bagh, the government appointed a commission of inquiry. The members of the Hunter Commission unanimously condemned General Dyer's actions and recommended his dismissal. It ought to be noted, however, that in some sections of British society they considered Dyer a hero. One paper raised 26,317 British pounds for the general, and presented him with a golden sword for his role as "Defender of the Empire".[54]

(ii)   Kapur Singh, National Professor of Sikhism, stated (January 13,1980): *"those in control of the statutory Sikh Gurdwaras are not aware of Sikh doctrines and the nature of the institutions founded on them. The true position is that… there cannot be jathedars as long as the Khalsa is not sovereign. Who would sit on the throne except a sovereign person representing sovereign people? Who shall be the locus of such sovereignty unless he emerges and is recognized as such by the sovereign Khalsa? The S.G.P.C. is the creation of a government statute and is elected by a college of voters, which includes a large percentage of those who are not qualified to be called members of the Khalsa and, by and large, they vote either for money or for liquor or for their group and cliques. Can such an institution as the S.G.P.C. name or sustain a jathedar who is the protector of the immortal power infused in Khalsa?"*[55]

Chapter Two – The Face of the Guru

(i) By definition, the face of a Khalsa must be illumined with the inner light of devotion. In the words of Guru Nanak Dev Ji, "Those who earnestly meditate on God's Name, their face shines with dedication, and they inspire others also to be free of the drudgery of living thanklessly in the world." (Japji Sahib)

(ii) If God were ever to need a shave and a haircut, where would He go, and whom should He see?

(iii) The use of the beardnet among colonialized Sikhs compares with the previous habit among many Afro-Americans of 'straightening" their naturally kinky hair. In each case, there was an effort to compromise some distinctive physical attribute in order to win approval, and thereby gain power and influence, from the predominant race. Black Americans gave up the ordeal of regularly applying caustic chemicals to their hair when a new era of self-empowerment dawned in the early 1970's. Instead, they began to openly proclaim, "Black is Beautiful!" and to pride themselves on their exuberantly self-conscious "Afro" hairstyles.

Those post-colonial Sikhs who have yet to abandon their particular badge of mental enslavement might well consider the following. Sikh dharma has, over time, been served by numerous gifted painters and illustrators of its glorious heritage. They have served to indulge our visual imaginations, so that we might feel emotionally and spiritually one with the saintliness and sacrifice that has gone before us. Arguably, the most inspired painter ever to put a brush to canvas was Sardar Sobha Singh. He once went so far, using his virtually unassailable status as the foremost painter of the Sikh nation, as to paint Guru Nanak Dev Ji with a type of cap, rather than a turban. This was intended as a conciliatory gesture to sahajdharis.[56] However, no artist of any standing whatsoever has ever dared to create a depiction of Guru Nanak through Guru Gobind Singh with his beard stuffed in a ridiculous net. Artistic indulgence has its limits! And if a beardnet looks wrong on the Sikh Guru, how can it look right on a Guru Sikh? Those who manufacture double standards befool themselves.

Chapter Three – Dressing for Imperialism

(i)   With the passage of time, it became abundantly clear that the fashions emanating from the haute couture salons of Paris, via London, not only failed to serve the cause of Sikh self-determination; they compromised the dignity and self-respect of any woman who wore them. Fashions were increasingly designed to expose the female form as much as to clothe it.   High heels, short skirts, low-cut blouses, and gauzy fabrics all were designed to meet the emerging needs of Western women. With the breakdown of traditional family structures in the Europe and American, women there were increasingly left to their own devices in the timeless pursuit of "finding and catching a husband".[57]   The young Sikh woman, whose marriage was still arranged for her, chose instead to dress in a style that expressed her modesty and enduring values, rather than depicting her as an alluring source of temporary sexual fascination.

Chapter Four – Her Majesty's Purveyors of Narcotics

(i) According to a nineteenth century British historian, William Lecky, the East India Company's agents "defied, displaced, or intimidated all native functionaries who attempted to resist them. They refused to permit any other traders to sell the goods in which they dealt. They even descended upon villages, and forced the inhabitants, by flogging and confinement, to purchase their goods at exorbitant prices, or to sell what they desired to purchase, at prices far below the market value… Monopolizing the trade in some of the first necessities of life, to the utter ruin of thousands of native traders, and selling those necessaries at famine prices to a half-starving population, they reduced those who came under their influence to wretchedness they had never known before."

A Parliamentary committee investigating the East India Company estimated that from 1757 to 1766 the company had drained more than 5,900,000 pounds from the treasury of Bengal through obligatory grants and bribes. In addition, there were the private fortunes amassed by many company functionaries, plus the firm's own revenues, out of which it maintained an army of mostly native troops, and sent home a yearly dividend of ten per cent to its stockholders.[58]

A further measure of the desolation exacted by Britain's trader adventures in their beachhead on the Bay of Bengal may be gleaned from two portraits of the principal city of Dacca. In 1757, Clive of Plassey, the military officer and administrator who subjugated and governed the territory and its people for George III, described the import center as "extensive, populous, and rich as the city of London". By 1840, however, official records reported that its resident population had fallen from 150,000 to 30,000. Sir Charles Trevelyan, then Permanent Secretary of the British Treasury, testified before the House of Lords that "jungle and malaria are fast encroaching… Dacca, the Manchester of India, has fallen from a very flourishing town to a very poor and small town." It is now the capital of the bustling, but economically backward, state of Bangladesh.[59]

The subject of the East India monopoly's profligate ways might have taken heart had they known that in 1773 C.E., some thousands of miles away, in Britain's Thirteen American colonies, certain rebel Englishmen were refusing to support both the high-handed Company and the Crown that gave it legitimacy, by boycotting its ill-gotten tea. From newspapers, pulpit and printing press came exhortations against the East India Company tea. Committees of freedom-minded colonists laboured overtime, preparing a common resistance. American physicians who had been won to the anti-tea cause warned that the drink "weakened the tone of the stomach, and therefore of the whole system, inducing tremours and spasmodic affections." They claimed drinking tea would make Americans "weak, effeminate and valetudinarian for life". One essayist warned, "Do not suffer yourself to sip the accursed, dutied STUFF. For if you do, the devil will immediately enter into you, and you will instantly become a traitor to your country." A New Yorker wrote of the East Indian Company, "It is shocking to Humanity to relate the relentless Barbarity, practised by the Servants of that Body, on the helpless Asiatics, a Barbarity scarce equaled even by the most brutal Savages, or Cortez, the Mexican Conqueror." In Philadelphia, the harbour's watchmen were advised to "Beware of the East-India Company" when they made their rounds.[60]

(ii)   Caffeine intake has also been associated by today's health professionals with migraine headaches, peptic ulcers, fatigue, high blood pressure, glaucoma, epilepsy, immune system suppression, heart disease, learning disorders, infertility, breast disease, gall and kidney stones, osteoporosis, pre-menstrual tension, and obesity.[61]

(iii) To this day, some Punjabi households prepare a beverage of spices boiled in milk, which is commonly referred to as "garam jal" (literally "hot water") or "desee chaee" (Indian tea), as opposed to "pardesee chaee" (foreign tea). In the West, a version of this beverage is marketed and sold by the name "Yogi Tea".

Chapter Five – The Jobs of the English

(i)   As far as real education went, the incidence of literacy in the Sikh kingdom had been higher than in some British provinces.[62]

(ii)   Baba Maharaj Singh's militant and uncompromising opposition to British rule in Punjab led the angrezees to apply particularly harsh measures to eliminate his "troublesome" influence. He was deported to Singapore on May 15, 1850 C.E. On the journey by sea from Calcutta, he was kept in a sealed cabin. After three years of solitary confinement, his eyes lost the ability to see. Three years later, he appeared to be little more than "a bundle of bones". Even a walk in the fresh air was not allowed to him. Finally, on July 5, 1866 C.E., he breathed his last.

Baba Ram Singh faced a similar fate. After it came to the knowledge of the British that he had sent missions to the kingdoms of Nepal and Hyderabad to explore the possibility of a joint action against them, he was arrested on June 18, 1872 C.E. The angrezees then deported the leader of the Namdhari Sikhs to Rangoon, where he remained until he left his mortal frame on November 29, 1884 C.E. His highly disciplined and motivated followers went on to make approaches to the Tsar of Russia and the then-exiled Maharaja Dalip Singh, to oust the foreigners from Punjab. The British so feared the Namdhari influence that they kept the successive leaders of the movement under continuous house arrest until 1922 C.E.

(iii) The secularizing influence of the English affected not only the Sikhs. None were more disturbed than the deeply tradition-bound brahmins. The Hindu priests naturally resented the work of Christian missionaries and the Government's support of converts. The brahmins were particularly bothered by the secular Englishman's vulgar habit of acting oblivious to time-honoured social distinctions. The priests did not appreciate that, under angrezee law, their special legal status had been removed, meaning they were no longer exempt from capital punishment. The brahmins also looked with disfavour on the English notion that women and men were to be treated as one, which caused widow remarriage and sati to be forbidden. They disapproved, as well, of the Englishman's emphasis on public schooling and the building of new urban colonies, and roads and railways from one end of the country to the other. The brahmins recognized that all these innovations would lead to an unprecedented intermingling of people from all social classes, without due regard for the dignity of the dignitary or the holiness of the holy. The brahmins had a particular dislike of the English habit of digging canals all over the countryside to irrigate more and more crops for some paltry earthly recompense, for in so doing they had diverted the water of the sacred Mother Ganges from their unerring sacred course.[63]

Chapter Seven – A British Education

(i) The Quaida Noor contributed to a phenomenal literacy rate in Punjab. After the defeat of Punjab, however the British were as keen to gain possession of these literacy devices as they were to find and confiscate any arms their citizens might retain. Not a single Quaida Noor is known to survive today. Indeed, documentation of the existence of Quaida Noor is scarce to non-existent. Robina Shoeb gained her knowledge of the device from the Fakir Khana family and cites Leitner as saying that "the war of 1857 destroyed this very useful practice and tradition, far superior and effective to what Europe then had to offer."[64]

Chapter Eight - Conclusion: "Angrezeemat"

(i) Angrezeemat especially influenced the protocol inside Gurudwaras established by Sikh men outside of India in places with sizeable immigrant populations like England, Malaysia, Singapore, Hong Kong, Kenya, Uganda, British Columbia and California. There, it was not unusual to find the established customs of "shoes off, turban on" and "pangat", the communal sharing of the food of the Gurudwara kitchen while seated in rows on the floor, displaced by habits that were distinctly English. Where the influence of Western customs proved stronger and Sikh traditions weaker, "langar" began to be served on tables while the congregation sat on chairs with their shoes on. Under the secular ideology, heads that were shaved and shorn, and sometimes without any head-cover, became increasingly common in these "modern" Gurudwaras. These temples were also invariably governed according to Western democratic traditions, following a pattern established in the major Sikh institutions of Punjab in the late 19th century C.E.

GLOSSARY

Akali Dal (Punjabi) – the "Army of the Eternal", traditional political party of Sikhs. Its roots are in the Gurudwara reform movement and the anti-Government agitation of the early 1920's.

Akal Takhat (Punjabi) – the "Eternal Throne, traditional seat of Sikh temporal authority, situated in Amritsar adjacent to the Harimandir. It was established by the Guru Hargobind Ji (the Sixth Guru) in 1606 C.E.

angrezee (Punjabi) – **1** English. **2** English-speaking.

angrezeemat (Punjabi) – the Englishman's understanding, derived from "angrezee" + "mat", or understanding.

avant garde (French) – those who set the trends.

Guru's Bana (Punjabi) – graceful, noble, distinctive garb of the Khalsa, consisting of kurta, pajama, turban, and the five K's, often in blue, but also in saffron or white.

C.E. – "current era" or, alternatively, the "Christian era" referred to as "A.D." (Anno Domini, Latin for "year of our Lord") by Christians. Its numerology commences with the traditional year of the birth of Jesus Christ. There exist today Chinese, Hebrew, Moslem, Hindu (Bikrami and Saakaa) and Sikh (Nanakshahi and Khalsa) systems of reckoning years, each with their own sacred starting point.

C.E. has been used in this work only because it is the favoured system in most of the English-speaking world. It is not, however, to take for granted that this is a truly Christian era in which we live. The times are clearly changing. For Sikhs, the Nanakshahi calendar begins in the year of Guru Nanak Dev Ji's birth, while the Khalsa era starts with the momentous events at Anandpur Sahib, when the order of Khalsa was established.

chadar (Punjabi) – a long cloth wrapped around a man's legs as clothing.

chuni (Punjabi) – a long scarf for covering a woman's head.

farangee (Persian-Punjabi) – foreigner.

five K's - the five designated symbols worn by every Khalsa; In Punjabi, they all begin with a "K". They are *Kes* (long hair), *Kangha* (a wooden comb), *Kachera* (breech-like underwear), *Kirpan* (a dagger or sword dedicated to the defence of life and honour), *Kara* (steel bangle).

gora (Punjabi) – a "light-skinned" person. This may be a derogatory or complimentary term, depending on how it is used.

Gurmatta (Punjabi) – a resolution arrived at by a number of dedicated Sikhs in the presence of Siri Guru Granth Sahib.

Gurudwara (Punjabi) – literally the "Guru's Door"; a Sikh temple.

Guru Gobind Singh Ji – the Tenth Guru of the Sikhs (1666-1708 C.E.). He established the Order of Khalsa and invested Siri Guru Granth Sahib with the authority of Guruship in perpetuity.

Guru Khalsa Ji – this term describes the oneness of Guru and Khalsa. Guru Gobind Singh infused Khalsa with the highest of human aspirations, a profound self-concept, and an empowering self-discipline. In essence, there is no more distinction between Guru and Khalsa than between Guru Nanak in any of his ten successive manifestations (Second, Third, Fourth, Fifth, Sixth, Seventh, Eighth, Ninth, Tenth Guru, and Siri Guru Granth Sahib).

Guru Nanak Dev Ji – the First Guru of the Sikhs (1469-1534 C.E.). He travelled widely, inspiring people to Truth and higher awareness. His greatest gifts to humanity are his Gurbani, the Sacred Verses revealed to him, and his successor, the Second Guru, an "ordinary" Sikh whom Guru Nanak inspired and trained to be worthy and capable of continuing his Mission, and leading the growing community of Sikhs.

kameez (Punjabi) – a loose kind of dress, worn by a woman over salwaar.

Khalsa – see "Guru Khalsa Ji"

kurta (Punjabi) – a tunic.

Michelangelo – renowned Italian sculptor and painter (1475-1564 C.E.).

moortee poojaa (Punjabi) – the Hindu practice of worshipping sacred images.

on the continent (British English), - on the European mainland.

panchayat (Punjabi) – an ancient system of local government in India, consisting of a council of five respected community members. Guru Gobind Singh breathed new life into the institution of panchayat when he founded the Khalsa, and glorified the Five Beloved Ones (*Panj Piaaray*).

pajama (Punjabi) – pants that are tied with a drawstring at the waist, snug at the ankles and loose at the thighs and hips.

sahajdhari (Punjabi) – an "easy-going Sikh", one who does not adhere to the Khalsa discipline.

salwaar (Punjabi) – a woman's loose-fitting pants, which are gathered at the ankles.

sarovar (Punjabi) – a pool of water associated with a Gurudwara, especially the one surrounding the Harimandir Sahib.

Siri Guru Granth Sahib – the Guru of all Sikhs, consisting of the Inspired Verses of Guru Nanak and many like-minded saints, including Hindus and Moslems. It was compiled by Guru Arjan Dev Ji (the Fifth Guru) in 1604 C.E., and made Guru by the Tenth

Master, Guru Gobind Singh, in 1708 C.E.

urban colony (Indian English) – translates into American English as "suburb".

William Blake – a visionary English poet, painter, designer and prophetic thinker (1757-1827 C.E.).

BIBLIOGRAPHY

Ali, Imran, *The Punjab Under Imperialism 1885-1947*, Oxford University Press, Delhi, 1949.

Bailey, Beth L., *From Front Porch to Back Seat – Courtship in Twentieth-Century America*, The John Hopkins University Press, Baltimore, 1988.

Bajwa, Fauja Singh, *The Kuka Movement*, Motilal Banarsidas, Delhi, 1965.

Bal, Sarjit Singh, *British Policy Towards the Punjab*, J.N. Sinha Roy, New Age Publishers Pvt. Ltd., Calcutta, 1971.

Bali, Yogendra, and Bali, Kalika, *Warriors in White*, Har-Anand Publishers, New Delhi, 1995.

Bhagat Singh, *A History of the Sikh Missals*, Punjabi University Publications Bureau, Patiala, 1993.

Bhagat Singh, *Sikh Polity in the 18th and 19th Centuries*, Orient Publishers and Distributors, New Delhi, 1978.

Chand, Tara, *History of the Freedom Movement in India, Volume I*, Ministry of Education, Government of India, New Delhi, 1965.

Chomsky, Noam, *World Orders Old and New,* Columbia University Press, New York, 1994.

Dilgeer, Harjinder Singh, *The Akal Takhat,* Punjabi Book Company, Jullunder, 1980.

Encyclopaedia Britannica, University of Chicago, Chicago, 1973.

Fairbank, John K., Reischauer, Edwin D., Craig, Albert M., *East Asia: Tradition and Transformation*, Houghton Mifflin Company, Boston, 1978.

Fauja Singh, *Some Aspects of State and Society Under Ranjit Singh*, Master Publishers, New Delhi, 1982.

Gopal Singh, *A History of the Sikh People (1469-1988)*, Second edition, World Book Centre, New Delhi, 1988.

Grewal, J.S., editor, *The New Cambridge History of India – The Sikhs Of Punjab*, Cambridge University Press, Cambridge, 1990.

Grewal, J.S. and Banga, Indu, *A Political Biography of Maharaja Ripudaman Singh of Nabha (1883-1942): Paramouncy, Patriotism, and the Panth*, Oxford University Press, New Delhi, 2018.

Gupta, Hari Ram, *History of the Sikhs, Volume IV*, Munshiram Manoharlal Publishers, Pvt. Ltd., New Delhi, 1982.

Gurdarshan Singh, "Origin and Development of the Singh Sabha Movement: Constitutional Aspects", found in *The Singh Sabha and Other Socio-Religious Movements in the Punjab 1850-1923*, edited by Ganda Singh, Punjabi University Press, Patiala, 1973.

Hamilton, C.J. *Trade Relations Between England and India*, Idarah-I Adabiyat-I, Delhi, 1975.

Hsu, Immanuel C.Y., *The Rise of Modern China*, Second Edition, Oxford University Press, London, 1970.

James, Lawrence, *The Rise and Fall of The British Empire*, Little, Brown and Company, London, 1994.

Kapur Singh, *Parasaraprasnas*, edited by Piara Singh and Madanjit Kaur, Guru Nanak Dev University, Amritsar, 1989.

Kashmir Singh, *Sikh Gurdwaras Legislation (All India Perspective)*, Singh Brothers, Amritsar, 1991.

Khushwant Singh, *A History of The Sikhs, Volumes 1 and 2*, Oxford University Press, Delhi, 1991.

Kumar, J. *Company India: A Comprehensive History of India (1757-1858)*, Janaki Prakashan, Patna, 1980.

Kumar, Ram Narayan, and Seiberer, George, *The Sikh Struggle*, Chanakya Publications, Delhi, 1991.

Warner, Sir William, *The life of the Marquis of Dalhousie, K. T.,*

Macmillan and Co, London, 1904.

Leitner, Gottlieb Wilhelm, *A History of Indigenous Education in Punjab Since Annexation and in 1882*, Republican Books, Lahore, 1882/1991.

Madanjit Kaur, *The Golden Temple, Past and Present,* Guru Nanak Dev University Press, Amritsar, 1983.

Madanjit Kaur, *Painter of the Divine – Sobha Singh*, Guru Nanak Dev University Press, Amritsar, 1987.

Malcolm, Lieutenant-Colonel, *A Sketch of the Sikhs, Their Origin, Customs and Manners*, Vinay Publications, Chandigarh, 1812/1981.

Malik, Ikram Ali, *The History of Punjab 1799-1940*, Neeraj Publishing House, Delhi, 1983.

Marenco, Ethne N., *The Transformation of Sikh Society*, Heritage Publishers, New Delhi, 1976.

Martin, James E., editor, *The Alternative Health Medical Encyclopedia*, Visible Ink Press, 1995.

Mathur, Y.B., *British Administration of Punjab (1849-1875)*, Surjeet Book Depot, Delhi, n.d.

Merbach, Melwyn, M.D., *Healing Through Nutrition – A Natural Approach to Treating 50 Common Illnesses with Diet and Nutrients*, Harper-Collins, New York, 1993.

Mohinder Singh, *The Akali Struggle – A Retrospect*, Atlantic Publishers and Distributors, New Delhi, 1988.

Mukherjee, Ramakrishna, *The Rise and Fall of the East India Company*, Monthly Review Press, New York and London, 1974.

Nahar Singh and Kirpal Singh, editors, *Rebels Against the British Raj, Volume II*, Atlantic Publishers and Distributors, New Delhi, 1995.

Narain Singh, *Jathedar Kartar Singh Jhabbar*, Singh Brothers, Amritsar, 1988.

Narang, A.S., *Storm Over the Sutlej – The Akali Politics*, Rise Press, Delhi, 1983.

Oxford English Dictionary, Volumes I-XX, Second edition, Clarendon Press, Oxford, 1989.

Pannu, Harjit Singh, "Village Police in the Punjab (1902-47)", from *Punjab Historical Conference 19th Session March 22-24 1985 Proceedings*, edited by Gurbachan Singh Nayyar, Punjab Historical Studies Department, Punjabi University, Patiala, 1986.

Prasad, Bisheshwar, *A History of Modern India (1707-1947) Volume I: Bondage 1707-1858*, Rajesh Publishers, New Delhi, 1981.

Punjabi University Punjabi-English Dictionary, Publications Bureau, Punjabi University, Patiala, 1994.

Sahni, Ruchi Ram, *The Struggle for Reform in Sikh Shrines*, Sikh Ithas Research Board, S.G.P.C., n.d.

Shoeb, Robina, "Refocusing on the Education under the Sikh Rule," *Journal of the Punjab University Historical Society,* Volume No. 30, Issue No. 2, July-December 2017, pp. 159-166.

Smith, Page, *A New Age Now Begins – A People's History of the American Revolution, Volume I*, McGraw-Hill Book Company, New York, 1976.

Yalland, Zoe, *Traders and Nabobs: The British in Cawnpor 1765-1857*, Michael Russell Publishing Limited, Salisbury, England, 1987.

Online Resources

Wikipedia

Battle of Ferozeshah

Delhi Durbar

Salute State

Maharani Jind Kaur

Maharaja Duleep Singh

1850's in Western Fashion

Edwin Samuel Montagu
Indian Tea Culture
History of Opium in China
Jammu-Sialkot Line
Sikh Regiment
Martial Race
Blowing from a Gun
Aitchison College
Bengal Famine of 1943
Partition of India

Other

Clock Tower of Amritsar: Casting a Long Shadow livehistoryindia.com

The Lost Palace of Amritsar sikhmuseum.com

Rani Jindan's Prayer book bl.uk

The Opening of the Sirhind Canal at Rupar bl.uk

---

[1] abridged from: Hari Ram Gupta, *History of the Sikhs, Vol. II*, pp. 54-5; Gopal Singh, *History of the Sikh People*, p. 374; Khushwant Singh, *History of the Sikhs, Vol. 1*, pp. 125-6.

[2] Kapur Singh, *Parasaraparasna*, pp. 247-8.

[3] Khushwant Singh, *A History of the Sikhs, Vol. 2*, pp. 416-7.

[4] M.L. Ahluwalia, Foreward to *Rebels Against the British Raj, Vol. II*,

p. xii.

[5] Sarjit Singh Bal, *British Policy Towards the Punjab*, p. 30.

[6] J.S. Grewal, editor, *The New Cambridge History of India – The Sikhs of Punjab*, p. 135.

[7] Narain Singh, *Jathedar Kartar Singh Jhabbar*, p. 31.

[8] Mohinder Singh, *The Akali Struggle – A Retrospect*, p. 14.

[9] *Encyclopaedia Britannica, Vol. 3*, p. 326.

[10] Mohinder Singh, *The Akali Movement*, p. 147.

[11] *Punjabi University Punjabi-English Dictionary*, p. 481.

[12] Ganda Singh, *Life of Banda Singh Bahadur*, p. 141-2.

[13] Ganda Singh, pp. 142-3.

[14] For the illustrious life details of the Sikhs listed here, who are not so well known in the West see Punjabi University's *Encyclopedia of Sikhism*.

[15] Oxford English Dictionary, Vol. III, p. 294.

[16] *Ibid Vol. I*, p. 952.

[17] Kalika Bal, Yogendra Bal, *The Warriors in White*, p. 75.

[18] Fauja Singh Bajwa, *The Kuka Movement*, p. 183.

[19] Khushwant Singh, *Vol. 2*, p. 120.

[20] Ruchi Ram Sahni, *Struggle for Reform in Sikh Shrines*, p. 103.

[21] Ramakrishna Mukherjee, *The Rise and Fall of the East India Company*, p. 301.

[22] Mukherjee, p. 301.

[23] C.Y. Hsu, *The Rise of Modern China*, p. 221.

[24] Hsu, p. 225.

[25] *Encyclopaedia Britannica, Vol. 21*, p. 738.

[26] *New Standard Encyclopedia, Vol. 4*, pp. 14-5.

[27] *Encyclopaedia Britannica, Vol. 21*, p. 738.

[28] Khushwant Singh, *Vol. 2*, p. 120.

[29] Hari Ram Gupta, *History of the Sikhs, Vol IV*, p. 524.

[30] Gupta, p. 526.

[31] Lieutenant-Colonel Malcolm, *Sketch of the Sikhs*, pp. 102-3.

[32] Fauja Singh, *Some Aspects of State and Society Under Ranjit Singh*, pp. 143-4.

[33] *Ibid.*, pp. 142-3.

[34] Y.B. Mathur, *British Administration of Punjab (1849-75)*, p. 17.

[35] Bajwa, p. 182.

[36] Khushwant Singh, *Vol. 2*, p. 120.

[37] Robina Shoeb, "Refocusing on the Education under the Sikh Rule," *Journal of the Punjab University Historical Society*, Volume No. 30, Issue No. 2, July-December 2017, p. 163.

[38] Gottlieb Wilhelm Leitner, *History of Indigenous Education in Punjab*, p. 150.

[39] Shoeb, p. 164.

[40] Ram Narayan, George Sieberer, *The Sikh Struggle*, pp. 99-100.

[41] Y.B. Mathur, *British Administration of Punjab (1849-75)*, pp. 79-89; M.L. Ahluwalia, Foreward to *Rebels Against the British Raj, Vol. II*, p. xii; J.S. Grewal, editor, *The New Cambridge History of India – The Sikhs of Punjab*, p. 130.

[42] Bishewar Prasad, *Bondage and Freedom, Vol. I*, p. 395.

[43] Tara Chand, *History of the Freedom Movement in India, Vol. I*, p. 197.

[44] J.S. Grewal, editor, *The New Cambridge History of India – The Sikhs of Punjab*, p. 130.

[45] Bajwa, p. 183.

[46] Ramakrishna Mukherjee, *The Rise and Fall of the East India Company*, pp. 420-421.

[47] Gurdarshan Singh, "Origin and Development of the Singh Sabha Movement's Constitutional Aspects", article in *The Singh Sabha and Other Socio-Religious Movements in the Punjab 1850-1925*, edited by Ganda Singh, p. 50.

[48] Mohinder Singh, *The Akali Movement*, pp. 8-9.

[49] Humayun Kabir, In Introduction to Bajwa, *The Kuka Movement*.

[50] Lawrence James, *The Rise and Fall of the British Empire*, p. 223.

[51] Adams, *Episodes of Anglo-Indian History*, quoted in Kapur Singh, *Parasaraprasna*, p. 247.

[52] Kapur Singh, *Parasaraprasna*, p. 249.

[53] Khushwant Singh, *Vol. 2*, p. 39.

[54] Gopal Singh, *A History of the Sikh People*, p. 650.

[55] Harjinder Singh Dilgeer, *The Akal Takhat*, pp. 91-2.

[56] Madanjit Kaur, *Painter of the Divine – Sobha Singh*, Section III, plate 26.

[57] Beth L. Bailey, *From Front Porch to Back Seat – Courtship in Twentieth-Century America*, especially pp. 3-24.

[58] Page Smith, *A New Age Now Begins – A People's History of The*

American Revolution, Volume I, McGraw-Hill Book Company, New York, 1976, p. 374.

[59] Noam Chomsky, *World Orders Old and New*, Columbia University Press, New York, 1994, p. 115.

[60] Smith, pp. 373-6.

[61] James E. Martin, editor, *The Alternative Health Medical Encyclopedia*, pages 159-60; Melwyn Merbach, M.D., *Healing Through Nutrition – A Natural Approach to Treating Fifty Common Illnesses with Diet and Nutrients*.

[62] Khushwant Singh, *Vol. 2*, p. 93.

[63] Zoe Yalland, *Traders and Nabobs*, p. 239.

[64] Shoeb, p. 164.

www.ingramcontent.com/pod-product-compliance
Lightning Source LLC
Chambersburg PA
CBHW042314150426
43200CB00004B/37